DAY TRADING STOCKS THE WALL STREET WAY

Founded in 1807, John Wiley & Sons is the oldest independent publishing company in the United States. With offices in North America, Europe, Australia, and Asia, Wiley is globally committed to developing and marketing print and electronic products and services for our customers' professional and personal knowledge and understanding.

The Wiley Trading series features books by traders who have survived the market's ever changing temperament and have prospered—some by reinventing systems, others by getting back to basics. Whether a novice trader, professional, or somewhere in-between, these books will provide the advice and strategies needed to prosper today and well into the future.

For more on this series, visit our Web site at www.WileyTrading.com.

DAY TRADING STOCKS THE WALL STREET WAY

A Proprietary Method for Intra-Day
and Swing Trading

Josh DiPietro

WILEY

Published by John Wiley & Sons, Inc., Hoboken, New Jersey.
Published simultaneously in Canada.

For general information on our other products and services or for technical support, please contact our Customer Care Department within the United States at (800) 762-2974, outside the United States at (317) 572-3993 or fax (317) 572-4002.

Wiley publishes in a variety of print and electronic formats and by print-on-demand. Some material included with standard print versions of this book may not be included in e-books or in print-on-demand. If this book refers to media such as a CD or DVD that is not included in the version you purchased, you may download this material at http://booksupport.wiley.com. For more information about Wiley products, visit www.wiley.com.

Library of Congress Cataloging-in-Publication Data:

DiPietro, Josh, 1976–
  Day trading stocks the Wall Street way : a proprietary method for intra-day and swing trading/ Josh DiPietro.
      pages cm.——(Wiley trading series)
  Includes bibliographical references and index.
  ISBN 978-1-119-10842-9 (cloth)   ISBN 978-1-119-15050-3 (pdf)
ISBN 978-1-119-15049-7 (epub)
1. Day trading (Securities) 2. Electronic trading of securities. I. Title.
  HG4515.95.D567 2015
  332.64′2–dc23
                                                                          2015019105

Cover Design: Wiley
Cover Image: Wall Street Buildings © JavenLin / iStockphoto

Printed in the United States of America
10 9 8 7 6 5 4 3 2 1

CONTENTS

Author's Note   xi
Three Essential Prerequisites   xiii
Introduction   xv
Discovering Day Trader Josh   xxv
Acknowledgments   xxxvii

PART I   MASTERING YOUR MINDSET BEFORE
            YOU ABSORB THE SYSTEM BY DAY
            TRADER JOSH   1

LESSON 1   Control of Emotions and Mastery
            of Focus   3

LESSON 2   How Overconfidence Can Destroy
            Your Trade   6

LESSON 3   Dealing with Your Impatience   8

LESSON 4   Knowing When to Stop Trading   10

LESSON 5   Risk Management: Buying Power
            versus Capital   12

LESSON 6	**Avoiding Overexposure to Market Risk**	**15**
LESSON 7	**Budgeting Your Way to Profitability**	**18**
LESSON 8	**A Realistic Look at Stop-Loss**	**20**
LESSON 9	**Day Trading Is *Not* Gambling**	**23**
LESSON 10	**Consistency Rules!**	**26**
LESSON 11	**News versus Noise**	**28**
LESSON 12	**When It Comes to Averaging Down, Amateurs Beware!**	**31**
LESSON 13	**What Stocks to Trade and Why**	**33**
LESSON 14	**Picking the Right Online Broker**	**38**
PART II	**DAY TRADER JOSH'S INTRA-DAY TRADING METHODOLOGY**	**43**
CHAPTER 1	**Basic Procedure**	**45**
	The Best Stocks to Trade with My System	45
	Additional Reasons Why You Should Take Only 15 Cents on Each Trade	49
CHAPTER 2	***Prior* Price Levels and Newly Forming Intra-Day Levels**	**53**
	The Basics of One-Minute Candlestick Chart Reading	55
	Get Your Daily Price Levels Logged and Organized	67
	What to Do After You Have Your List of Daily High Price Levels and Daily Low Price Levels	68

Log Your *Prior* Price Levels on a
Whiteboard *Before* the Opening Bell   70

Now You Start the Five-Candlestick
Counting Process   74

How to Count Five Minimum
Candlesticks (Chart Analysis)   75

Notes, Reminders, Cautions, and Hints
of the Lessons to Come   76

**CHAPTER 3   Intra-Day Golden Rules:
Entry/Exit Setups   78**

The Rules Explained   79

Mastering the Three-Tier Max Strategy
with 100-Share Block Trades   84

Understanding the Wisdom of 15-Cent
Static Profits   86

Observing the Framework of Entry and
Exit Strategy with Step-by-Step
Procedures and Guidelines   88

Entry Strategy   90

Exit Strategy   91

The Wisdom of Using Strategy Stop-Loss   92

**CHAPTER 4   The Mechanics of FASTKEY Order
Execution   96**

Using Your Keyboard Keys for Rapid
Order Execution   96

Placing Orders Directly from a Level 2
Quote Chart (Direct Access)   97

Executing Real-Time Trades (Manual
Limit Orders)   100

Scrutinizing Both Real-Time and
End-of-Day Trades with Back-Testing   102

CONTENTS

PART III   DAY TRADER JOSH'S SWING TRADING
             METHODOLOGY   **107**

CHAPTER 5   **Introduction to Swing Trading:
             Basic Rules and Procedures**   **109**

             Introducing the Ten-Day Hold Rule   111

             How to Determine the First-Tier Swing
                Level   112

             Understanding Entry and Exit Setup
                Rules   115

             Two Key Swing Rules to Follow   118

             Buying Power and Trading Experience
                Dictate Your Swing Strategy   121

             Here's the *Good* News!   122

CHAPTER 6   **Sample Swing Charting Setups**   **124**

             The 5 Percent Bubble   126

             Swing Trade Setups   129

PART IV   THE *FUSION* OF INTRA-DAY AND
             SWING STRATEGIES   **137**

CHAPTER 7   **Introduction to Fusion Trading**   **139**

             Why Are They Not Mutually Exclusive?   140

             Applying the Golden Rules   144

             Deciding Your Trading Options:
                Intra-Day Only, Swing Only, or
                Fusion?   148

CHAPTER 8   **Sample Fusion Trade Setups**   **150**

             Sample Fusion Trade #1   152

             Sample Fusion Trade #2   156

             Sample Fusion Trade #3: An Advanced
                Fusion Trade   160

             Final Words on Fusion Trading   169

CONTENTS

PART V   ADVANCED RULES AND PROCEDURES   171

CHAPTER 9   Maximizing Net Profits and
Minimizing Losses on Overall
Trade Setups   173

What Is Pivot Trading?   175

Sideline Trading   178

Earnings Release Trading   181

PART VI   TRADING AND TRAINING WITH DAY
TRADER JOSH   187

CHAPTER 10   My Trading Room and How
It Works   189

CHAPTER 11   The Day Trader Josh Training
Program   195

Program Details   196

Learning Objectives   197

What the Price Includes   199

Recap   199

About the Companion Website   200

My Final Words to Readers:
Warnings, Reminders, and
Prospects for the Future   201

Index   207

ix

Caution!

Alone, this manual will *not* adequately teach you my intra-day trading and swing methodology. Your mastery of my system will only come about through formal hands-on training.

Much of what you'll find in this sequel is material from my training manual. Graduates of my program will tell you that there's much more to learning my system than reading text or looking at one-dimensional charts.

As with any other line of work, mastery requires your guidance for weeks, if not months, by a veteran. If you think you can simply read about a method and then apply it to real markets with success, then you're in for an ugly shock. I say this because I've made that mistake, and I don't want it to happen to you.

In my first book, *The Truth About Day Trading Stocks*, I discuss the harsh realities of applying a new method without any hands-on training. Whether you're a greenhorn or you've been trading the markets for 20+ years, getting the gist of any real day trading system demands more than just reading a book or watching a few day trading webinars or seminars.

So I repeat: don't attempt to trade any of the procedures and/or rules mapped out in this book. This is only a framework meant to give you an idea of what's ahead. This is the map, not the road.

My goal here is to show you what my system can do for you, and also how much is involved. *This system is not easy. This book is not a how-to.* This book is your introduction. It's meant to reveal why my training program lasts for one full year. As with any real trading system, applications and real-world procedures come into play as you develop your competency. This requires weeks of hands-on training with a real day trading coach.

Do not attempt to trade with this system without formal training from me.

■ Do Not Read Out of Order!

I specifically designed this book to read as a technical manual. All material is critical to read in order, starting with the Cautions page. If you do read out of order and jump to certain sections, you will only make the material that much harder for yourself to fully digest. So please start reading from here and enjoy!

THREE ESSENTIAL PREREQUISITES

1. Don't perceive day trading as a quick alternative to make fast cash. You go into this as you would in any serious attempt to take the time and make the effort to learn a real profession.
2. If you're planning to trade fulltime, you need to acquire a *pay-per-share* broker. This is a broker who charges *no more* than $1.00 per 100-share block trade.

    (*Note:* If you're only planning to trade part-time, and you'll be focusing on swing trades that produce more profit potential than intra-day trades, then most *pay-per-trade* brokers will suffice. You don't have to consider changing online brokers until you've been formally trained.)
3. You do not need to open or fund a live account while training with Day Trader Josh. Once you begin to real-trade, however, you will need a minimum starting balance of 25K.

This amount is a bylaw imposed by the SEC. When you're intra-day trading stocks, and you're placing more than four roundtrip trades in any five-day rolling period, you're considered a *pattern day trader*. As such you must fund your account with no less than 25K.

If your balance falls below that amount, you get hit with an *equity call*. This means you can't trade on margin or pattern day trade until you deposit enough funds to return your balance to 25K.

> You do not need to open or fund a live account while training with Day Trader Josh.

If you've read my first book, *The Truth About Day Trading Stocks*, then you're well-prepared for this new, more technical application of my trading methodology. Before you get started, all you'll need is awareness of the updates and modifications that have been added since 2008, and that vital information is here.

For those who haven't read *The Truth About Day Trading Stocks*, I recap the book's major lessons in the first part of this book.

I designed this second book specifically to disclose my proprietary applications to intra-day trading stocks and swing trading stocks (equities). I have been trading since 1998, but I learned most of the applications here while trading on private equity floors near Wall Street. After I disengaged from private equity trading floors I began my own unique system that works for the relatively lower-capitalized independent day trader. After eight years of testing and trading with a high rate of success, I finally designed my own highly transparent trading system.

In this book I show you precisely how I trade stocks by using both intra-day and swing strategies, and most importantly, by using their *fusion*. You will be introduced in Part 4 to my new term, *Fusion Trading*.

What is *Fusion Trading*? Think about it: you can't place an intra-day trade without knowing where your swing levels are. Conversely, you can't place swing trades without considering your intra-day levels. That interconnection is the core of my system and the secret to the Wall Street price levels: no guesswork, no indicators—nothing but *real* price levels. Your challenge is to know which price levels work best for you, and how many shares at each level.

You may be tempted to apply what you learn here to live trades. That would be a huge mistake. Just reading about the system will not make you ready to use it. My goal here is to have you digest the information and see the potential for success, a potential that can't be realized until after I've formally trained you.

> This system is not easy to learn. That's why this system works.

The importance of hands-on training can't be overstated. As a survivor of life-shattering Crash & Burn, I am one trading mentor who cares whether you profit or plummet. I was once a victim of those big-box training programs that gouge your credit card, herd you in like underfed cattle, corral you for a couple of days, and then throw you to the wolves of Wall Street.

That won't happen here.

In Part 1, I address the permanent, ironclad focal points of *The Truth About Day Trading Stocks*. You'll find instructions that must be hardwired into your trading psychology. These are prerequisites to learning the framework of my intricate current system. Hundreds of rules and procedures must be followed to the *T*.

The biggest potential for disaster is real, live trading with only the framework learned here. Don't be that guy who tries one portion, say 1 percent of my system, loses money, and then posts online that my system doesn't work. I know that guy exists and I'm trying to prevent you from becoming another one. I do care about the outcome for anyone who is trading my system.

In Part 2, I introduce you to *only* the intra-day portion of the system. It's critical that you start with intra-day, because you need to get in rhythm with your stock on that basis. I show you which level to trade, and why. You'll learn several procedures and the *mechanics* of intra-day trading. You'll learn why it's crucial to not assume that you can trade the intra-day rules and strategies without knowing the swing trading system, and without knowing how to fuse them.

In Part 3, you'll learn the core swing trading methodology. Again, you'll see why you can't use one strategy without thoroughly knowing the other. The fusion of both is shown later.

In Part 4, you will be introduced to Fusion Trading. I show examples of several trade setups that illustrate how important it is to know both intra-day and swing trade strategies. You'll find that you have several options, such as intra-day trading only, swing trading only, or intra-day trading and swing trading on the same day.

In Part 5, I offer several advanced rules and procedures. One is what I call *pivot trading*. I use this method to recapture any incremental losses in one single trading day due to a stop-loss exit on a portion of my overall position. I show you how, at the very next trading session, I get right back in at the same level or better.

In this part I also show you what I call *trading from the sidelines*. In essence this is when you have a predetermined entry price in mind, but for whatever reason you missed the entry, and then the price goes lower or higher in your favor. What do you do? I demonstrate several scenarios and options.

The most risky time of year to trade, especially when you're not formally trained, is earnings season. Four times a year, your stock exhibits extreme volatility. I have several strategies and procedures that can help you capitalize on huge runs, earning far more than the normal day-to-day swing trade. I also establish rules that keep you safe and on the sidelines.

In Part 6, I demonstrate several examples of how you can easily screw this system up by throwing certain rules out the window. My main goal in this part is to drive the point home that this system takes weeks if not months of training with me before you are ready to go live. If it were up to me and not my editors, I would title this part: *The Guy Who Thought He Could Trade This System without Being Formally Trained*.

Sorry, I remember my own foolishness, so I know it has to be said.

This part is an eye-opener. I show that there are so many variables that it's suicide to apply this system in static mode, meaning, you can't apply certain rules across the board; certain situations require different actions, and you have to change price levels in real-time.

This part gets into what I call the *poor training factor*: applying what you can't learn on paper after only having tried it on paper.

Even trainees in my one-year program still make mistakes, so you can just imagine how much trouble you'll get into without any hands-on experience. Those mistakes are mapped in this part. They are a gory sight.

In Part 6, I show you the differences between a bogus trading room and a trading room that actually shows *all* entry levels *before* they hit. Most importantly, you'll see the danger of following a trading room when you haven't yet mastered the system. For instance, just because I'm entering at a certain price level and a certain amount of shares does *not* mean that you should do likewise at that exact time. This takes much explaining to make sense. After Part 6, you'll understand.

I also show you screenshots of my own trading room and explain how it works and what to expect when you're using it to trade my system.

Also in Part 6 you get a sneak peak at my training program and how it works. You may have a gazillion questions. I address them in this section, and I repeat that the material here can't prepare you for live trading, and I show how my one-on-one training program does.

The only true way to get your questions and concerns answered is mentorship from a day trading veteran. Again, this book is not designed to prepare you to start applying my system with real money. It offers you a look at the framework.

■ Changes and Updates Since My First Book (2008)

Any viable day trading system must be updated and adapted to market trends and changes in rules and/or regulations. Since 2008, when I published *The Truth About Day Trading Stocks*, we've seen the biggest bull market in history. This combined with the proliferation of high-frequency trading systems and the virtually zero-interest-rate FED policy has created more volume in the stock market than ever before. Due to high volume and liquidity, stocks have been moving much faster. Because of those factors, I no longer trade primarily the smaller intra-day setups, as I did in 2008. I've been compelled to orient my system more toward swing positions.

This *does not* mean that you, as a beginner, should *not* be trading intra-day levels. In this book as well as my training program, I instruct you to start *only* with intra-day levels. I have you observe the strongest levels, but for the time being, do nothing more than watch. The main reason for this is safety. You won't be holding intra-day positions overnight. It makes no sense to do so and it's way too risky.

Even under my coaching, and especially when you first go live, I'll have you trading only intra-day setups. Eventually you'll graduate to riskier yet more profitable swing trades; meanwhile, you should only take baby steps.

Because I've altered my system, and because of the higher price levels on the type of stocks I now look for, I've increased my stock price criterion to a minimum of $100 and a maximum of $250. I elaborate on this later.

High-frequency trading systems have basically taken over Wall Street. For the small guys, this means the intra-day levels are not as dependable as before. By "small guys" I mean the average novice trader. You have to be more conservative now and the levels you pick more extreme.

Unless you have your own trading group and black box (high-frequency trading computer with direct access to Level 2 quotes and powerful trading software), and millions, if not billions, of dollars, then you have to tread very carefully when trading in this new market. This is why I invented the *Fusion*. This is the trading of strong swing levels in conjunction with the strong intra-day levels. It's much safer to trade this way now. I still trade off intra-day levels, but what I use now are very defined and strong intra-day levels. I no longer trade "intermediate" intra-day levels. Those are the newly forming levels that are created *between the intra-day high and low* on any given day. Those levels simply are not dependable anymore—they are very risky to trade.

Changes and Updates Summary

- Now I primarily swing trade—*Fusion Trade*.

- My new system works *only* when trading stocks between $100 and $250.

- I can now hold positions overnight, but *only* if I'm in a swing trade.
- I allow profits to run for at least $1.50—in some cases $5+.
- I now trade the day after earnings, off earnings price levels.
- My training program has grown from two weeks to one full year.
- I now offer "Golden Rules" for intra-day setups.

■ The Breakdown

- Now I primarily swing trade.

This is by far the most fundamental change to my system. I started swing trading when I realized that the normal intra-day levels are no longer dependable with my established three-tier setups system. I do still use that system, but now I only utilize specific price levels. This will be explained in the intra-day part of this book.

In *The Truth About Day Trading Stocks*, I stress the importance of not *holding* overnight. I state this at least 50 times. For the beginner, that rule remains ironclad. If you're new to this system, you won't be holding overnight until you learn the swing portion. Only swing trades can be handled that way, and only if the price levels and rules in my system dictate that you can do so.

I've also found that once you know your swing level, you can start intra-day trading whenever you're within *roughly* $3 of it. I explain that in detail later on. What I want to clarify now is that, while swing trading has become the more profitable and dependable price level to trade, intra-day trading remains a good strategy while you wait for the stronger swing trades to hit. I started using both systems because I found how much they complement each other. As a matter of fact, they're interdependent. Here's how: you need to know your intra-day levels in order to get a precision swing entry, and you need to know your swing levels in order to pick your proper intra-day levels. Separating the two is like the blind leading the blind.

The thing to keep in mind is that swing trading is the most advanced part of my current system. As a beginner, you should only intra-day trade until you have more expertise. You'll make very little in profits, and you'll run the risk of having to stop-loss at the close, but I'd rather have you safe than sorry, and not holding overnight, until you master my system.

Mastery means you're swing trading, or what I like to call *Fusion Trading*. I introduce you to my full system in Part 4, which details my new and time-tested Fusion Trading system.

- My new system works *only* when trading stocks between $100 and $250.

As I mentioned previously, the bull market has pushed most of the stocks that work with my system to well above $100. Therefore, I've had to adjust it to work with higher-priced stocks between $100 and $250. In *The Truth About Day Trading Stocks*, I stress the importance of starting with $10 stocks and working your way up to $50, then $100. This is for intra-day trading only, and *only* for practicing when demo trading. (Even in that original training program I was using $100 stocks, but that was because I knew how to trade them. The entire theme of my first book is about keeping you safe with low risk as you learn, especially if you're not under my mentorship.)

I get this question all the time from traders who are reading my first book: "Does your system still work with $10 stocks?" I always respond that it has never worked, not unless you *like* waiting all day for a 15-cent profit ($15). Some third-world citizens earn more than that in one day!

Think about it. Low-priced stocks only have intra-day price ranges of 10 cents to at most $1. You would not make much at all if trading this system with stocks priced under $100. Not to mention you would need to trade more than 100 shares on each position, thus driving your pay-per-share commission through the roof. Again, teaching trainees to trade with $10 stocks is only for training purposes.

The most consistently traded stocks are priced in the $100–$250 range. We day traders know consistency is everything. If you're ever queried about this, here's a good way to respond: "We need stocks over $100 simply because they move fast and have high volume, and most importantly, because they're very liquid. And we don't want stocks over $250, because they move too fast and take up way too much of our capital." During the stock-picking portion of this book, I pinpoint the stocks in that range.

- I can now hold positions overnight *only* if I'm in a swing trade.

As I've mentioned before, *holding* overnight was a huge no-no when I started coaching intra-day trading. The term *intra-day* says it all: those newly formed levels are meant to *only* last that day. The only safe exceptions are the levels that have formed on a *daily* chart, meaning previously established levels that have held for several days to form strong support and resistance price levels. Those strong levels are proven pivot points that under certain circumstances can be held overnight for a profit the next day or even further out.

I can't tell you how many times I've had graduates of my original training program contact me while tearing their hair out, wondering what to do next, after they've held weak intra-day position trades overnight. Here's what I always say:

> Stop-loss now—you screwed up! Bite the bullet and don't *ever* do that again.

If any of you who have done that are reading this, you know you broke the Golden Rule of intra-day trading. Hopefully by now you can look back and laugh.

But here's the thing. If you learn to apply my new system, entering at a well-established *swing* price, then the Rule no longer applies. Those levels are much stronger than an intra-day level and in many cases *should* be held overnight.

Yes, with my upgraded system, you do the forbidden: you *hold overnight*. You just have to know when you can, and I clarify this later. Meanwhile, I can't say it enough: *this new book is only the framework*. You don't want to attempt my new system with real money until I've formally and properly coached you.

- I allow trades to run for at least $1.50 in profits per 100 shares—in some cases $5.00+.

This update is pretty straightforward. I reemphasize that the $1.50 minimum profit on a trade only pertains to a swing position.

Again, only swing trades can profit more than 15 cents per trade. The new swing levels you'll see in this framework will be extremely strong levels, enabling you to sensibly take more profits. In certain cases $5+ can be a profit. For instance, trading strong levels *after* earnings release can be very lucrative.

When I mention huge gains it's exciting, but if you don't use this system properly—don't have it taught to you properly—you can easily lose $5+ on the trade, and then you have to stop-loss because you picked the wrong levels at the wrong time and had the wrong amount of shares. It took me years to learn when to take more or less profits, and how many shares at certain levels. So many variables come into play. I chart the majority of them in this book, but it's up to you to remember that this is just the map, not the road.

- I now trade the day after earnings, off earnings price levels.

If you don't have a solid trading system in place, and you don't stick to your rules, then earnings release dates are by far the most dangerous times to be trading. Though I have an established system for trading during earnings season, my new swing system allows for you to enter a trade the day *after* an earnings release. Yes, I wait till Wall Street decides what the highest and lowest price will hit just after earnings release, and then I trade off those price levels the next day. This is the only time you can capitalize on much larger profit runs.

Of course, I can only show the framework here, with only one example, and that's like showing aliens a human and saying every human is its clone. The point is: each stock trades differently and at different speeds, so you really have to know your stock if you're out there trading off earnings.

Accordingly, here's one part of the Golden Rule that hasn't changed, and never will:

I never hold a position overnight into earnings release.

- My training program has grown from two weeks to one full year.

Because the most risky time to trade is earnings season, I decided that the best way to help you master my system is to have you remain in my program for an entire year. That way you receive four real-world experiences with earnings release dates. Whether you're trading one stock or ten, you need my coaching during these four periods each year. Without a doubt, earnings season is the most active time in the markets. Even my graduates still struggle with getting this period correct.

Many of you have already been under my training, some in my initial two-week program, then in my four-week program, and finally in the six-week program that covers the entire core training. In the past I've offered to coach for a whole year, and found that most traders either don't want to pay my tuition fee or simply believe they've learned enough to do it on their own. The truth, however, is that the longer my trainees remain with me, the better they tend to do. Most graduates who haven't stayed under my wing are likely not doing so well. I've surveyed several and found that two common denominators have led to their downfall: (1) earnings season wiped them out, and/or (2) they threw half my rules out the window.

When trading under my watch, you don't make those mistakes, not without my literally yelling at you to stop. And now that my program lasts much longer, you have months to gain skills under my supervision. Mastery of this system comes with months of live trading while watching my trading rooms and questioning me in real time on setups—both entries and exits. There is no fast-track formal training.

Do lawyers squeeze their training into measly four-week courses and then take on murder trials? Law school takes three years for a reason.

■ I offer Golden Rules for intra-day setups

I will be explaining the new Golden Rules in Part 2. Essentially, these short and easy-to-remember directives will keep you in a trade until it profits, or will keep you out and safe on the sidelines.

■ How I Trained, and How I Journeyed Closer to Wall Street

My journey began back in 1998, in sunny San Diego. I caught a free trading seminar and learned that it's possible to sit in my shorts and make tons of money online, buying and selling stocks at home. I opened a traditional online day trading account through a prominent pay-per-trade broker. Back then, I was paying about $14.99 per trade.

I also found out how easy it is to lose a lot of money very fast. I began searching for day trading academies. I purchased every relevant book I could find. I was desperate to learn how to profit consistently.

I found a three-day intensive trading program in Irvine, CA. It cost $6,500. It offered no guarantees, but the lunches were free! The trader/instructor who sold me over the phone was very convincing. He promised I would learn some proprietary information that would catapult my day trading to glorious new heights.

After the three-day program I came home to my trading station. At the time it was two laptops and a 36-inch Gateway monitor. I felt like a truly professional trader. My confidence level was through the roof.

To make a long story short, I lost so much money within one year that I had to sell my house. I also almost lost my fiancée.

I was a mess! I had to take a break from full-time day trading. I searched for some kind of small business for myself in order to pay the bills. I started a mobile car detailing business and quit actively day trading for about three years.

I did maintain my online brokerage account, and I did place several "guesswork" trades during my three-year hiatus. I never made much money, especially consistent money, until I decided to get back in again, actively trading intra-day.

It was 2004. I was finishing up my bachelor's degree in Business Marketing from San Diego State. The rigors of college were helping me become a much smarter and more resourceful person—and most of all, more patient.

I came into some money, and this encouraged me to give full-time day trading another chance. I purchased a few current day trading books, and decided to dish out another $5,000 on my second professional trading program (a different trading academy from the first one).

This program was a five-day intensive and professional trading program (or so they promised). Once again I drove up to Irvine. I expected to be taught a highly structured way of profiting consistently in trading equities.

Once again I was let down. And this time, it was even worse. The program didn't teach me anything that I didn't already know. I felt completely ripped-off.

I continued to day trade with my traditional pay-per-trade account until 2006. I was moderately successful with a pay-per-trade broker and trading platforms. The best thing I got from that period was learning how the stock market truly functions. I got to where I was trading more than four roundtrip trades in any five-day rolling period. This much activity defined me as an official "pattern day trader." The SEC requires all pattern day traders to have at least 25K in their brokerage accounts.

I had no problem with that. My problem was the pay-per-trade commission structure. That was killing me. I was placing over 10 roundtrip trades per day. That's 20 executions per day. That translates to $200 in commission fees per day ($9.99 per trade). I needed to find a way to trade without getting charged so much per trade.

The year 2006 was key. That was when I began to seek out pay-per-trade firms with much cheaper per-trade commission costs. The lowest I found was $4.99 per trade. That was still too high.

At about the same time I'd got intensely curious about the day trading firms in New York City. Some of them offered a commission structure that was unfamiliar to me: pay-per-share. The more I researched pay-per-share, the more I knew I had to move to New York City. I found that there were literally hundreds of small, independent private equity trading floors.

They each had different criteria for entry and different capital investment amounts, but they all had the pay-per-share structure—the fees ranged from 30 to 80 cents per 100-share block traded. That translates to paying only pennies on the dollar for each trade. I only needed 100-share block trades because I was trading stocks highly priced at the time, $50–$100.

Most of the independent pay-per-share trading firms were on or near Wall Street, so I sold everything I owned and relocated to Manhattan. Now I lived 30 blocks away from Wall Street. I was blown away by those firms. They all had their own trading floors. The caliber of experience of the day traders there made me feel like an amateur. And the truth is, compared to those veterans, I was. For two years I was exposed to real day trading firms and real day traders. I learned more than I had in all years prior. *Everything I know to date is in this book.*

My Style of Trading: Both Intra-Day and Swing Trading—The Fusion of Both

I am defined as an Intra-day trader and a Swing Trader, but as I've mentioned before I now call myself a *Fusion Trader.*

Intra-day trading is the specialty of taking profits on small price changes, generally soon after a trade has been entered and has become profitable. It requires you to have a strict exit strategy, because one large loss could eliminate the many small gains that you've worked to obtain.

> You never hold an intra-day trade overnight.

Swing trading is basically trading off levels found on the daily chart, much stronger levels than intra-day levels. Therefore, you allow your profits to run further because your entries are off extremely overbought/oversold price levels.

I position myself at my trade station each morning, starting at 8 A.M. (or 5 A.M. on the West Coast). I usually trade only the first two hours. But if I'm looking to enter/exit a Swing position, then I watch the charts all day. I watch and trade a max of *five* stocks per session (up to *ten* for swing).

Whenever I'm intra-day trading, I typically start my trading positions in 100-share blocks. I will allow a position to grow to 300 shares maximum (and more if it hits swing levels). On a productive day (trading all day with both intra-day and swing trades) I will place about 60 executions, or 30 roundtrip trades (when trading all my stocks).

When swing trading, the amount of shares and how many price levels I accumulate varies depending on several factors that will be addressed later on in this book.

In my program, you will be practicing and learning with *one stock only*. Once you're on your own, you will eventually progress to trading two, three, four, and a max of five stocks simultaneously. The more stocks you can trade, the more trades you will place, which generates more profits.

In this book you will be learning both my intra-day and swing strategy. You will find that I currently primarily trade swing levels; you, too, will eventually gravitate toward swing once you master the system after I have trained you.

The Direct Market Access Provider I Use for Order Execution and Data Feeds

I use the Lightspeed trading platform for my fastkey order execution (direct market access). Lightspeed offers FASTKEY order execution capabilities. This means you can use your arrow keys and function

(Fn) keys on your keyboard to place orders (I will be teaching you the framework to FASTKEY order execution later in this book).

Lightspeed also has all the data feeds you could possibly need. It provides all the basics, such as customizable charts and analytical indicators. Basically, Lightspeed is a one-stop-shop for all your day trading needs. And of course, they are a pay-per-share commission-based brokerage firm.

Most important, Lightspeed has a pay-per-share structure. Depending on your trading activity you could be paying anywhere from 40 cents to $1 for a 100-share-block trade, great for intra-day trading.

The Amount of Capital and Leverage (Buying Power) This System Requires

As both an intra-day trader and swing trader, I enjoy a good range of trading options. The benefit of intra-day trading is that relatively little trading capital is needed in order to day trade stocks/equities. With swing trading, however, the sky is the limit. How much capital I have to invest determines the amount of shares and price level. This will be explained in greater detail in the swing section of this book.

When it comes to intra-day trading, think about it: if you're trading a $100 stock in 100-share blocks, then you only need $10,000 to trade that position. If that's not enough, then you may want to trade 5 stocks at once, and then you only need $50,000 to trade all similar positions.

Either way, you don't need hundreds of thousands of dollars to become a professional day trader. By SEC regulations, you only need $25,000 to open an account.

Here are the main benefits to being a *pattern day trader*:

- Initially, you're given 4:1 leverage. You open your account with $25,000 and you have $100,000 in buying power.

- You can place as many intra-day trades as you want.

- You should be paying $1 or less on each 100-share block trade.

Early Morning Preparations

I usually wake up around 6 A.M. (5 A.M. if on the West Coast). While having my coffee I begin my current market news observations. I like to browse websites like Bloomberg.com and the Yahoo Finance section. Once I have my trade station all lit up, I click on the TV. I watch CNBC. In my opinion, this business channel is the best for observing market-moving headlines. Once I've digested the market news, I focus my attention on my stock list. I begin filtering through each stock on my watch list. I usually have about 5 to 10 familiar stocks to watch on any given day (you will soon learn how I select stocks). I'm looking for any news that can potentially hurt my stock, or make it extremely volatile that day. If my stock is making headiness, then I will not intra-day trade it, but will swing trade it.

If I deem that the stock should trade normal on this day, then I add it to my Today's Trade List. That's my whiteboard on the wall.

All my early morning preparations lead into the opening of pre-market trading. Once I get up, I usually have an hour before the pre-market trading session opens at 8 A.M. EST.

Most amateurs and even novice traders don't realize they can execute orders, not just place them, starting at 8 A.M. EST. This is another advantage of trading through a pay-per-share broker. *But no one at the amateur level should try it.*

Pre-Market Trading

Pre-market is 8:00 A.M. to 9:30 A.M., before the opening bell. At 8:00 A.M. the Level 2 quote charts start to move and orders begin to fill. The charts start dancing across the screens.

During this period I'm watching for any abnormal activity in my stocks. I'm also keeping track of any breakouts—pre-market stock prices breaking through the previous day's high and low price before the 9:30 A.M. opening.

Basically, I need to log what price levels hit during pre-market trading. That way, I can have a true documentation of the highs and lows of the day (pre-market prices are not logged on most intra-day Level 2 quote charts).

The Opening Bell

When the bell rings at 9:30 A.M., I am locked and loaded. I know exactly what *price levels* I'm using to execute trades for each of my selected stocks (you will soon learn how to determine these price levels).

If I'm *actively* intra-day trading, I usually place at least 10–20 roundtrip trades in the first hour of trading. I like to be high energy and focused during the first hour of trading.

My trades are quick and decisive. I now take exactly $15 (15 cents) in profits on each intra-day trade, meaning, if I have a 300-share closeout-full position, then profits are $45 on the three-tier setup trade. But I *always* begin my trade in 100-share blocks, and this is how I will train you. In the morning, I trade 1 to 5 stocks simultaneously.

Note: In Part 4 you will learn my Fusion trading system. I actually make $1–$2+ on each intra-/swing trade, on *all* my trades, but you, as a beginner, will take 15 cents on intra-day trade setups. This will be thoroughly explained later on.

Once I quickly execute a trade, I am quickly looking to exit with a small profit (using FASTKEY). I *never hold* intra-day trades past the close (unless it becomes a swing trade). I *always* make 15-cent profits on intra-day setups.

Midday Activities

By 10:30 A.M., I've executed about 10–20 trades. I usually take a quick 10-minute break after I've closed out all positions.

Once I have taken my break I begin some research on my performance. I'm gauging which stocks I want to stop trading for the day and which stocks I plan to continue trading. I choose the stocks that have been consistent in their volatility and price movements (this will be described in greater detail later).

Around lunchtime I wind down. I close all my positions and take my break, usually 45 minutes. I tend to stop trading around 12 P.M. EST. I will begin again around 2 P.M., if I feel like it. This is different if I'm in a *swing* trade.

Keep in mind: about 75 percent of all intra-day trades happen in the first two hours of the market. This is why I now *only* intra-day trade up to 11:30 A.M., although I do place *swing* entry/exits all day, if applicable.

After lunch I usually decide to shorten my stock watch list. I try to trade only one to three stocks leading into the close. After trading and watching all my original stock picks for the day I begin noticing fairly consistent trends in a few stocks. Again, I may be swing trading a stock or two.

The Last Hour of Trading

The market usually picks up volume and volatility during the last hour of trading. After 3 P.M., I'm always on high alert. I save the last hour for my best performing stock all day. Whichever stock has been trading like clockwork I will stick with until the bell rings.

The key to the last hour of trading is *not holding* any large positions. I don't have to worry about this because I never trade in more than 300-share blocks (on intra-day trades). During the final hour I will limit my exposure even more by not trading more than 100-share blocks at any given time. This way, when the bell rings at 4 P.M., I will only need to close out a 100-share block position.

The Closing Bell

Ding-ding-ding-ding! At 4:00 EST the U.S equities markets are closed. The workday is done.

No it is not! I always sit at my trade station for at least another hour. I like to watch how my stocks trade in after hours. I like to watch how after-hour news affects the markets and other stocks. And, of course I like to gauge my profit/loss performance for the day.

Homework

Whether I'm working from home or on the trading floor, I like to call it homework. After I'm completely closed out of all my positions for the day, then it's time to recap my performance.

I start by focusing on the best and the worst trades of the day. I like to simplify the screening process by utilizing the following essentials:

- Stock symbol
- Amount of shares purchased on individual trades
- Total Amount of shares
- Long/short position
- Time of entry

- Time of exit

- Profit/loss

- Number of total trades

Taking time to recap is crucial. It makes me slow down and think about my trading style. Trading styles have to be constantly updated, just like a computer.

In order to be able to gauge your trading performance, you must go back and research what happened at the time you executed the order.

These days I research my intra-day trades and focus on the following primary errors:

- Was my original entry price the correct intra-day S/R level?

- Did I simply falter at the FASTKEY?

- Did I tier into the 300-share position properly?

- Did I hesitate on initial breakout and then chase trade?

- Was I impatient and frustrated at time of entry?

- Was I simultaneously in more than one trade?

- Can I view the entire trading session on one screen?

- What obvious mistake(s) can I remember having made?

- Most important: Did I use the Golden Rules (learned later in this book)?

Upon answering these questions, I walk away feeling more in control of my trading style. Now I can relax and enjoy my evening, feeling better about my performance.

One Full Virtual Trading Day with Day Trader Josh—*Swing Trading*

Early Morning Preparations

Same as Intra-day, I usually wake up around 6 A.M. (5 A.M. if on the West Coast). The biggest difference is that I'm now focused on my swing room and the stocks that are within $3 of hitting in pre-market trading. Those will most likely be the stocks I will be swing trading today.

If I decide to, I will enter a swing before bell rings—a highly advanced strategy and not to be executed until you master this system.

Again, you can execute orders (not just place) starting at 8 A.M. (Eastern Standard Time). This is just one more advantage of trading through a pay-per-share broker. *But you will not be doing this anytime soon!*

Pre-Market Trading

Pre-market is 8:00 A.M. to 9:30 A.M., before the opening bell. At 8:00 A.M., the Level 2 quote charts start to move and orders begin to fill. The charts start dancing across the screens.

I am certainly watching pre-market trading; this is the one time-frame that both intra-day and swing levels come together. You will learn why later in this book.

For now just note that pre-market trading is the most relevant trading period leading into opening bell, meaning your high/low of pre-market is more important than your previous day's after-market high/low. I will be showing you how to use pre-market high/low when trading both intra-day and swing levels.

The Opening Bell

Whether I am intra-day or swing trading, when the bell rings at 9:30 A.M., I am locked and loaded. I know exactly at what *price levels* I am prepared to execute trades for each of my selected stocks (you will soon learn how to determine these price levels). When swing trading, I already know my entry levels because they have been in my online trading room for days, leading up to this moment.

On any giving day I can hit all or none of my swing levels. I typically have about eight stocks that I trade every day, for years, in some cases. But some stocks will not hit swing levels in as much as two to three weeks, and others can hit swing levels almost every day. It depends on the volatility of each stock. As you will soon see, my stocks are all highly volatility, especially when priced $100–$250 each. But still some may take longer than others to hit swing levels that I have previously determined.

So, there are days I just sit and wait and don't place one single swing trade, and then there are days that so many levels are hitting

I miss a few opportunities, and/or my capital was not sufficient to trade all levels.

I might enter a swing level; you will be taught that you need to take $200 profits on each 100-share block trade, that is, a $2 run for each swing level. I like to call swing levels "swing tiers."

Note: You will be taught in the advanced part of this book when/how to trade each level. For instance, should you wait for a lower second tier and skip first tier? Should you trade 100, 200, 300, or 500+ shares on each tier? These questions are the core of swing trading and ultimately my Fusion Trading system.

You will be very educated on this one premise after reading this book: just because I'm entering at certain levels and with a certain number of shares does not mean *you* should have traded at that same level and same amount of shares. In the past, I wrote a feature article in *Stocks & Commodities* magazine that explains how one trading room can actually be the worst thing for a novice trader to use. This will make more sense after you read the section on my trading room and how it works.

Unlike my intra-day system, with swing trading the sky is the limit once you master the entire system. Again, mastering can only be done when formally trained by the master of the system.

Midday Activities

Like intra-day trading, by midday when swing trading, chances are I am done for the day. No more levels are likely to hit after 1 P.M. But, if I'm in a swing trade and waiting for my $2+ profit target to hit, then I will be watching the price action all the way to the bell.

Again: about 75 percent of all swing *entries* (not necessarily full roundtrip trades) happen in the first two hours of the market. So, by midday I know the likelihood of any more swing levels/tiers hitting.

Last Hour of Trading

This is the same as for intra-day trading. The market usually picks up volume and volatility during the last hour of trading. After 3 P.M., I'm always on high alert. I save the last hour for my best-performing stock all day. Whichever stock has been trading like clockwork I will stick with until the bell rings.

The key to the last hour of trading is *not holding* any large positions. I don't have to worry about this because I never trade in more than

300-share blocks. During the final hour I will limit my exposure even more by not trading more than 100-share blocks at any given time. This way, when the bell rings at 4 P.M., I will only need to close out a 100-share block position.

When swing trading during the last hour, you have several decisions that must be made, especially if your position dictates you must hold overnight according to the rules you will soon be learning.

The last hour is just as busy as the first hour in most cases; it is the make-or-break period of day. I will be showing you several strategies that give you the best positioning to maintain a profitable trade when swing trading.

The Closing Bell

Ding-ding-ding-ding! At 4:00 EST the U.S equities markets are closed. The workday is done.

No, it is not! I always sit at my trade station for at least another hour. I like to watch how my stocks trade in after hours. I like to watch how after-hour news affects the markets and other stocks. And, of course I like to gauge my profit/loss performance for the day.

When swing trading, it is the same thing except I am updating my "daily levels" and my swing room. It's critical that I know my next tiers if I am holding a swing position overnight.

Homework

Homework is essential on every swing trade. My swing trading room needs to be fully updated at the end of each trading session. By updating the swing room I am recapping the levels I traded that day and planning my entries for next day.

ACKNOWLEDGMENTS

I want to thank my graduates and current trainees who trade with my system successfully and inspire me to fine-tune my coaching. Because of you, this new book developed, with all the new charts and rules for your safety and even more gainful procedures.

I'm also very grateful to professional day trading media outlets, such as the MoneyShow and TradersExpo and *Stocks & Commodities* magazine. Over the years, they've been very influential in the growth of my networks with fellow day traders.

And many thanks to Georgianna Groen. She colors my words with aplomb. Her editorship is superb. I'm a day trader, not a writer. We can all thank Georgianna for making my instructions both compelling and comfortable reading.

Mastering Your Mindset Before You Absorb the System by Day Trader Josh

Note: This section contains 14 generalized lessons based on the premise of my first book, *The Truth About Day Trading Stocks*. Each lesson includes updates and changes I've made since its publication in 2009.

Control of Emotions and Mastery of Focus

■ The Fear and Greed Factors

Nothing affects your trading behavior like these two disruptive emotions. You need to be aware of their influence whenever you're in a trade. The fear factor keeps you safe, but you make very little money. The greed factor tempts you with the *chance* to make a lot of money, but it usually just gets you in trouble.

Fear is a natural instinct. From birth, you're hardwired to avoid risk. But greed has the power to override fear and cause you to do things that you normally wouldn't. In day trading, fear and greed have to be squarely faced, always watched out for, and tamed. You can never totally apprehend their influence on your subconscious. No one is completely immune to these overwhelming impulses, but you can train yourself to resist them in each of your trading decisions.

■ How to Control Them

The way to keep fear from manipulating your performance is to limit your exposure. This is why I stress that you only trade in 100-share blocks, and sometimes less. With 100-share blocks you won't feel as much fear as when you're wrestling with 1,000-share blocks.

Suppose you're in a trade with 100 shares and the stock moves against you by a full dollar. You're only down $100, not so bad. But what if you're holding 1,000 shares? Then you're down $1,000. You will soon find that I trade stocks that can fluctuate one full dollar every minute. If you're a nervous wreck while trading a position, then most likely you're trading more than 100 shares per trade.

Other ways to avoid fear include:

- Not holding a losing position all day—*always* having an exit plan

- Not holding an intra-day position overnight because it closed in the red

- Not trading with your rent/mortgage money

- Not trading when you've been consistently losing for days—taking a break instead

If you find yourself unhappy with making small profits all day, then greed can start kicking in, and you can quickly get in way over your head. The way to avoid a disaster while sating your urge to trade more than 100 shares is to deliberately limit yourself to a maximum of *300* shares (three tiers) per trade setup whenever you're intra-day trading.

Other ways to avoid greed include:

- *Never* recklessly average-down a position. Trade *real price levels*.

- Avoid breaking your consistency. If you've been trading a certain way all day, *do not* start trading differently in the last hour.

- *Never* break the Golden Rules.

■ How to Stay Focused While Trading—*All Day*

Focus is the quintessential factor in the success rate of every day trader. Here are crucial ways to stay focused:

- Never take your eyes off your screens while in a trade, especially when it's an intra-day trade for 15 cents. That means no lunch breaks, no phone calls, no trips to the bathroom, and so on.

Before you engage in any activity that distracts you from watching your screens, you must close your positions, hopefully at a profit.

- Don't trade on a day when you have personal/family issues that will most likely cause you to trade on emotion.

- If you have a hangover, then wait until late afternoon to start trading. You don't have to start early in the morning.

- If there's a major national crisis occurring, and it's having an effect on the stock market, then you should take the day off.

- Drink coffee to stay alert, and exercise and stretch at your trade station. The exercise is especially effective because your blood circulation is improved. You'll be more energized, but also more calm, and you won't get fatigued and have muscle aches.

After I've trained you, if you don't stray from my system, you'll be a much better day trader. What I teach is very structured and procedural and will keep you on target and alert, that is, *focused*. Once you master this system, you'll know when you've made a mistake, and how. But most of all, you'll know when you're about to make a mistake in real time, and how to head it off, because you're *focused*.

How Overconfidence Can Destroy Your Trade

6

■ Confidence Is Great Until You Have Too Much

Overconfidence, like the greed factor, makes you take too many risks. But it's not about the itch for more profits. It's about getting too complacent with your trading style, or trying new trading strategies without testing them first on the demo (paper-trading). Worst of all, it's about trading this system that you see in a book without being formally trained in it.

Here are some typical indicators that you're trading with overconfidence:

- You place a trade with very little prior research—you just dive in.

- You stay in a trade past your predetermined exit points. You place a trade seconds *before* a major report is released, and you try to predict which way the market will respond (you're trading *into* an earnings release).

- You add more shares to your trade and don't have enough capital to hold overnight, and then you find yourself holding more than 300 shares in one single intra-day trade.

- You recklessly average down a trade and hold a losing position.

The telltale sign of overconfidence is inconsistency with profits and/or losses. For instance: you've been steadily making between $500 and $1,000 per day in profits, and then suddenly you're making or losing $3,000 per day. This means you've started trading outside of your consistency levels, and the reason is you're getting cocky.

Think about it. When you day trade, you must keep your levels uniform. That may sound boring and sometimes it is, but uniformity keeps you safe from reckless trading.

This will keep your confidence realistic:

- Only trade stocks that have passed the criterion-selection test (this I clarify later). Only trade them once you've tested them on your demo (paper-traded).

- Don't ever try to make "double" the amount on a trade—not until you're much more experienced.

- Stay highly consistent when trading: trade in 100-share blocks, and then slowly progress from there. That's what I teach in my program. If you jump right in and try to apply a new system to more than one stock and more than 100 shares, that's overconfidence. Your failure is practically guaranteed. You're spreading yourself way too thin.

- *Always use the Golden Rules*. Never stray from them. As soon as you do, you're trading on confidence and not trading the system—you're gambling.

In the past, some of my own biggest bloopers were seeded by overconfidence. If you're under my wing, I will not allow you to make my mistakes. You'll be way too busy struggling to apply all the rules and procedures and you won't have the time to get reckless.

Dealing with Your Impatience

■ Traders Have to Cope with Two Kinds

The hardest lessons a trader will learn usually result from impatience. In day trading, you deal with two forms of this weakness.

The first kind of impatience you're going to feel right out the gate, from your first day as a beginner. Most amateurs want to fast-track their way to pro-trader glory. What they don't understand is that the true road to success is about slowing down and taking the time to learn the deep skills of day trading.

Everyone wants to progress quickly in this business. The sad truth is that most beginners lose their start-up capital—at least once. Amateurs quickly get impatient when they can't keep their profits consistent. Finding the tolerance to deal with slow progress is too hard. It's not what they expected. Then they get reckless and lose.

The realistic way to see day trading is to picture a college student earning his Master's degree. It certainly takes patience—and years— to achieve a Master's degree. Why should becoming a pro-trader demand anything less from a person?

You feel the second type of impatience when you're down in the trenches of day trading, and you're learning to wait for your intra-day signals. *Intra-day trading patience* is what really counts in pro-trading.

You must have the ability to sit at a trade station with the focus of a lion that watches its prey.

Impatience, and all the losses that result, causes amateurs to crash and burn and give up. The good news is that, with my system, you're going to hit most price targets in the first two hours of the market. You need to be on high alert for only 120 candlesticks on the charts. Essentially, you're paying yourself to be patient for 120 minutes.

■ How to Control Your Impatience

Amateur Impatience:

- Don't expect to trade for income until you've practiced under the wing of a seasoned veteran. And even then, don't expect to make consistent profits or income. How well you do depends on how much training you receive and how much you apply what you've learned. This is like any other profession. You get back what you put in, and in order to make a big profit, what you put in must be skillful.

- Don't try to make huge profits on one single trade.

- Don't quit your night or weekend job.

Intra-day Trading Impatience:

- Get a really comfortable chair and trade in a lit-up atmosphere.

- Make sure your stocks match my criterion list (I clarify this later).

- Don't trade if you've had a couple of bad days in a row. Take a break and go back to demo-trading—practice without real money.

- Don't force trades because your target price isn't hitting. If your price target doesn't hit, then you have no trade. It's that simple.

Knowing When to Stop Trading

■ Why Taking Breaks from Day Trading Is Necessary

For any trader, pro or amateur, one of the hardest decisions to make is whether to stop trading for a while. Amateurs usually view this as surrendering, or giving up, but pro-traders understand that it's a necessary aspect of being a seasoned professional.

If you've been trading in the red for over three days, and your emotions are dictating your style and performance, then it's time to take a break. During your hiatus, however, you should remain very active in the stock market.

Later on I show you what I call "sideline trading." You're going to find that break-taking can actually make you more profits. While you're pausing and sitting on the sidelines, your stock prices can hit key high points that you otherwise wouldn't have waited for. Thus you can enter at much more desirable and profitable price levels.

If the fear and/or greed factors are running you, you will only make bad decisions. When you know this is happening it's in your best interest to stop for a few days, or even weeks, or even months. Then and only then can you find the right perspective and finally get back to the battlefield with new confidence and new focus.

■ What to Do During Your Inevitable Break(s)

- Go back and review every single trade you've ever made. Start with the largest losses and the biggest profits. Look for patterns. Find your core issues and deal with them. Usually the issues are mistakes that you *repeat*. Resolve to stop repeating them.

- Continue to watch your current stocks on an intra-day basis. Don't ever lose track of their performance and rhythms. Just because you stopped trading doesn't mean Wall Street did. That way, when you return to trading, you will still be in the loop.

- Reevaluate your financial situation. Create a new budget that will allow you to return to active trading without the bad emotions you left with. Lick your wounds and move on.

- Don't just jump back into active day trading. First, take a full week to demo trade (paper-trade). Get your rhythm back in a risk-free environment before going live again.

- Don't return to active trading with the goal of retrieving the money that you lost in your previous battle. That attitude and strategy will only bring on more disasters.

- Lower your expectations.

- Remember that each time you lose money in the stock market you've paid a high price for a very expensive and painful lesson, a mistake you will not make again.

> Taking breaks is all about understanding how to capitalize on those agonizing lessons.
>
> **From *The Truth About Day Trading Stocks***

Note: Lessons 5 through 9 deal with risk management, which is a critical factor that is grossly under-taught in most training programs.

Risk Management: Buying Power versus Capital

■ How Much Buying Power to Trade With

Capital is the amount of cash that you initially fund your account with. *Buying power* is how much leverage you're given by your broker. For instance, if you're given a 4:1 leverage, then your initial 25K capital investment gets you 100K in buying power. Your buying power determines how many shares you can purchase of any given stock.

You should only be trading with money you don't need for bills. The start-up capital you initially use to open your account should be investment money, not cash you need back right away. This is obvious, and it's not my emphasis here. Here I'm discussing how much buying power you should be trading with.

Much depends on whether you're intra-day trading or swing trading. But either way, in order to actively day trade with a 4:1 leverage or more, you must have at least 25K in your account *at all times*, because this is enforced by the Securities and Exchange Commission (SEC).

Do the math and it's plain to see that when you're *intra-day* trading you'll have at least $100,000 in buying power when you open an account with the minimum 25K. Does this mean you should be trading all of that buying power?

Of course not; as a beginner you should only be trading in *100-share blocks per trade*. If you're trading a $100 stock, then you only need $10,000 of your $100,000 in buying power. This is because you only need $10,000 to purchase a 100-share block to trade.

Once you get better at this, you'll start trading multiple positions. For instance, you'll eventually have an average of five stocks per day. At any given time you may be holding five separate positions, and each will be 100-share blocks. Therefore, you'll only need, on average, $50,000 in buying power to be trading those five positions.

Risk management really boils down to how you can control your consumption of the buying power in your account. Believe me, it's very easy to slip up and start recklessly trading a position, which means averaging down *recklessly*.

For instance, you start a trade with 100 shares of a $100 stock (using up only $10,000 of your $100,000 in buying power), but you quickly start purchasing more and more of the same stock. You can easily end up holding 1,000 shares of this $100 stock because your buying power allows you to do so.

Do you see where that can lead? Do you really want to be in a 1,000-share position while the stock is dropping precipitously? That's gambling.

Risk management can be kept in check by consistently trading in 100-share blocks. Self-discipline is obviously the key there.

On the other hand, when you're *swing* trading, you can trade with as much capital as you have in your account. In other words, the sky is the limit. Obviously you have to limit yourself while first trading this new system, and when I mentor you, I'll be making sure that you do. One of my major rules in swing trading is that you *do not hold* margin overnight. You can only hold as many shares as you have in cash capital. That rule alone keeps you very safe.

I coach both 25K account holders and the highly capitalized people who are well into the seven digits. I always tell the seven-digit people that just because they have millions of dollars doesn't mean they should start trading with that much right out of the gates. Those highly funded traders are often slower to get it than most of the moderately funded. My guess is that they take more risks and break more rules simply because they can. They're not losing their homes or going starving on the street, but they do get frustrated from losing.

So I alleviate this by having everyone practice in 100-share blocks on each position, no matter how much capital they have. Only when they prove that they're trading my system properly will I let them start upping the stakes.

■ Recaps on Managing Your Buying Power

- Once you fund your day trading account with 25K, you'll be given 4:1 leverage in buying power. *Do not use all of it.* You can ask for whatever amount of buying power you want. I suggest that you start your account with only 2:1, so you'll have 50K to trade with (or double your initial capital investment). Eventually you can ask for more, but for now you don't need it; it will only get you in trouble.

- Stick with five stocks that you know very well. Only trade them in 100-share blocks.

- Avoid averaging-down a position. Don't ever find yourself holding a single position that has *more than 300 shares*. That's especially true when the stock is over $100.

- When swing trading, just because you can afford 5,000 shares of a stock doesn't mean you should be trading it with 5,000 shares. Start with 100 shares per entry. Better to be safe than sorry.

Avoiding Overexposure to Market Risk

■ Normal Exposure Is the Amount You Can Lose—Overexposure Is Disaster

15

Normal exposure to the market usually refers to the amount you can afford to lose in a single trade. Overexposure occurs when you're not prepared for that loss.

Here are some causes of overexposure:

- You've purchased too many shares at one time without being used to the swings and the rhythm of the stock.

- You've purchased a stock at the wrong time of day, as in the first 15 minutes, pre-market, or aftermarket, when uncertainty is dangerously high.

- You're trading stocks that don't meet my stock-selection criteria.

■ Trading Consistently in 100-Share Blocks Prevents Overexposure

Trading consistently in 100-share blocks is the fastest way to learn how to trade at a profit. By trading in 100-share blocks per trade, you're eliminating any possibility of overexposure to market risk. Of course you're also limiting your profit, but as an amateur you need to forget about trying to get rich quick. You need to keep safe from big losses.

The key to trading in 100-share blocks is having a *pay-per-share* commission structure. Most *direct market access* (DMA) providers offer this structure (I elaborate this later). When you use pay-per-share you can place several intra-day 100-share block trades, and you don't have to worry about paying $9.99 per trade as you would in the *pay-per-trade* commission structure.

When you pay per share you can expect to pay about 40 cents to a dollar per trade. To get started you need to have a pay-per-share broker and the self-discipline to never get ahead of yourself by trading larger-share blocks per trade.

■ Recaps on How to Avoid Overexposure

- Open an account with a pay-per-*share* online broker. This allows you to trade in small-share blocks and avoid overexposure to market risks. (If you're ready to *only* swing trade, however, then having a pay-per-share broker may not be necessary. I explain this in the swing section.)

- When intra-day trading, only trade in 100-share blocks per trade, with a maximum of 300 shares from three-tiers/different price levels.

- Never try to trade on news and economic reports. Don't try to predict what Wall Street will do. As you learn my system you're going to realize that the news is already built into our price levels. Wall Street knows the news better than you and I do, so you should just trade the charts.

- Never trade stocks that don't pass my stock selection filtering process.

- Avoid trading in pre-market and aftermarket hours, especially as an amateur trader.

- *Never hold* an intra-day position overnight under *any* circumstances.

- If you're new to swing trading, *never hold* a position overnight if it's on margin. (In my program I allow this only when you've totally mastered the system.)

Budgeting Your Way to Profitability

It's worth repeating: the most common mistake most amateur day traders make is thinking they're going to advance quickly in day trading. Most amateurs lose most of their start-up capital within months of their first trade. You can avoid this by receiving proper training. My mentorship program helps you set realistic financial goals. I also help you keep your destructive impatience in check. I keep after that like a smoke alarm.

My goal in this lesson is to financially prepare you for the rough road ahead.

■ How to Stay Out of the Poorhouse

- Obviously it's essential to not quit your main source of income. Most of us mortals have to work for our hard-earned cash. If you happen to have plenty of savings, and you've deemed it investment (or *disposable*) income, then I guess you can ignore this advice. But to those of you watching your wallets, I can't say this enough: I hope you're aware of the danger of investing in a career that can wipe you out overnight.

My job as your mentor is to train you on how to not lose all your money. After you've learned that essential, only then will I allow you to work on consistent profits.

- It's best for you to have a job that doesn't require your attention during market trading hours, which are 8 A.M.–11:30 A.M. EST. It's ideal if you can work nights and weekends, or, if you live on the West Coast, you can start trading at 6:30 A.M. and be done by 8:30 A.M. PST.

- In the beginning do not expect to make consistent income from day trading. It will take you several months (or even years) to become a pro-trader who can rely on day trading profits for your consistent income.

- You need 25K to open a pay-per-share account, and I strongly suggest a cushion of an additional 5K. This is important because if you fall below the minimum 25K, then you'll be placed in an "equity call." This means you most likely will have limitations on your leverage/buying power, and you will need to immediately add funds to your account to get it back up to at least 25K. Therefore, the additional 5K helps you have peace of mind when you're first starting out.

The bottom line is that you mustn't be financially desperate when you're day trading stocks. Your starting capital should not be your life's savings or credit, or your kids' college fund. You should approach your start-up capital as you would any business investment: by planning, researching, budgeting, and with plenty of margin for error. Because even under my wing, and even after months of training, you can still slip up and make a classic mistake that will cost you your hard-earned dollars.

A Realistic Look at Stop-Loss

■ Stop-Loss Should Be Automatic

No day trader likes to place a stop-loss. But all pro-traders understand that it's a normal part of the day trading process. As I mentioned in the section on updates and changes, my current system redefines stop-loss and how or when you should execute one.

(For those who have been under my mentorship, I want to remind you again that I *no longer use* nominal value stop-loss exits. Now that I use swing trades as major pivot points, it makes absolutely no sense to stop-loss when I'm $XXX in the red. Instead I capture even stronger levels when accumulating a position. This I clarify later.)

Here I'll show some important uses of stop-loss in some very definable situations. There is never any guesswork with my system. I refer to this as *strategy stop-loss*.

■ How to Properly Strategize Stop-Loss without Hesitation

- Always have a predetermined exit strategy. *Never hold* an intra-day position past 4:00 P.M. at market close. *Never hold overnight*.

- If you accumulate more of a swing position intra-day and are using margin/leverage, then you must stop-loss the amount of shares on margin. (Later I introduce to you what I call *pivot trading*. This strategy allows you the opportunity to recapture the amount lost today on the very next market opening.)

- *Never hold* any position into an earnings release (typically in after-market trading). Exit your entire position by 4:00 P.M. on the day of earnings release. This is especially true for swing positions that you *can* hold overnight—just never into earnings release. It's way too risky to hold into a release, because once Wall Street starts trading, the stocks we trade can easily fluctuate $30+ in either direction. That's a $3,000 loss, even with 100 shares, if you get the call wrong.

- Never allow standard stock related news to dictate your entry/exit process, except when your stock is literally hitting the "breaking news" wire on the MSNBC channel. Combined with other factors, such as the volume on the stock and how many shares and which tiers you're in, only then should you think about just exiting when in the red. If you're in the green, that's great, but if not, that's a classic time to stop-loss.

The above almost never happens with my stocks. Most news is already factored into the price, so breaking news has to be truly in the moment and devastating or otherwise hugely impacting for me to stray from my plan.

A great example of this is what happened with TSLA, a stock of mine in 2014. A battery caught fire in one of Tesla's new cars. When that news broke, I immediately exited my positions on TSLA. A few days later I simply recaptured my loss by getting back in at lower levels and riding the price back up.

All this may sound easy, but believe me it is not. I only got back in because it was hitting the lower levels that I was planning for, regardless, which illustrates my point: you *always* have to know your price levels.

Other examples of strategy stop-loss would be a CEO giving notice of stepping down or when mergers are announced. Again, these things almost never happen with our $100+ stocks, so stop-loss caused by the news is very uncommon with my system.

The most prevalent reason for strategy stop-loss is actually the easiest to follow: *if you know you made a mistake by entering at the wrong price level, then stop-loss*. It's that simple.

After you learn the framework of my system, you'll have a much clearer understanding as to why I haven't stop-lossed when I've been $2, $5, or even $10 in the red. It wouldn't have made any sense. If I had, then many of my past profitable trades would have been losers to date.

My system is *countertrend trading*. This means that if I'm deeply in the red, the current price is that much more likely to reverse back into the green.

This is the critical reason why you've got to know *all* of your price levels—at any given time of the day—no guesswork.

Day Trading Is *Not* Gambling

■ There's a Huge Difference Between Them

In *The Truth About Day Trading Stocks*, I dedicate an entire chapter to the differences between gambling and day trading stocks. Here I recap how they're not the same, and also how they can become the same if you're throwing the rules out the window.

23

If you were to ask a pro-day trader whether he thought day trading was gambling, he would most likely respond with this question: "Are you referring to when I was an amateur, or to me as the veteran I am now?"

Without any proper training, amateurs are likely to gamble. Gambling boils down to the simple odds of winning or losing, nothing more. Gambling doesn't offer many options while your money's in play. Once you roll the dice in craps, and your bets are on the table, you can only sit back and fervently hope that your numbers land in your favor. You're casting your fate to pure luck.

On the other hand, when day trading stocks, you have many strategic options. If you skillfully utilize those options, your day trading will never be gambling.

■ Day Traders' Options *Not* Available in Casinos

■ You can add more funds as the stock price increases or decreases while you're still in the trade. Or you can simply wait on the sidelines for lower/higher/more favorable price levels to add to your position (this is *not* averaging down).

■ You can decide how much loss you can tolerate and how much profit you want by predetermining your stop-loss and limit price. You can alter these decisions while in the middle of a trade. Then you can recapture your losses at more desirable levels later in the day.

■ You can hold (intraday) your position until your stock price retraces in your favor.

■ You can tier into your position until it retraces.

■ Finally, there's the option of transparency. You have the ability to view stock charts and Level 2 quote charts. Chart analysis and stock research are key factors in your day trading success. Again, it's all about knowing your price levels.

■ How to Make Sure You're Day Trading, Not Gambling

■ Always predetermine your stop-loss and limit prices *before* entering each trade. *Stick to your original plan.*

■ *Do your homework.* Make sure your price levels are correct before the bell rings.

■ Only trade in 100-share blocks, and *never hold margin overnight* on swing trades.

■ Don't try to trade on news and/or economic reports; in other words, don't try to predict what Wall Street will do next.

■ Never start trading a new stock in large share blocks, like 200 shares or more. *Stick to 100 shares per trade on all new stocks.*

- If you've been trading in the red for a few days straight, *do not* try to go big and get your money back. Instead, take a couple of days off from trading and regroup. Also avoid day trading when something in your life is causing bad emotional swings.

- Don't ever trade because you "feel lucky."

> Luck is a gambler's best friend. Not needing luck is the day trader's distinction.

From *The Truth About Day Trading Stocks*

Note: Lessons 10 through 14 address general trading strategies.

Consistency Rules!

■ Stay Consistent in Your Trading Habits and Tactics

In intra-day and swing trading, consistency equals success. You can be consistent in losses, or you can be consistent in profits. The latter is a feat, the hardest thing to achieve, and it takes lots of hands-on practice. This is why I've evolved my training program to last for one full year. Considerable time is needed to master this intricate system.

Unfortunately, the hard way is the only way that works. You will learn from your own mistakes. My job is to help you minimize those errors, and to offer advice and strategies that will help you start profiting, sooner.

"How do I trade consistently?" you might ask. "I just sit at my trading desk all day, doing the same thing over and over, right?"

Actually, that's true. But it's not so easy to master. Here's how to *not* break your consistency.

■ Maintain a Highly Regimented Trading System

■ Trade the same stocks every day. Get to know your stocks the way you know your favorite songs—you know their rhythms and lyrics by heart. The longer you trade familiar stocks, the quicker you'll consistently profit.

- Keep your *share sizes* consistent on each trade. If you're trading 100-share blocks all day long, *do not* start trading in 500+ share blocks in the final hour of trading or at any other time of the day. This break in your intra-day consistency will affect your trading psychology. When you begin to trade erratically and overexpose yourself, your emotions will quickly get out of control.

- Keep your *profits* consistent on each trade. For instance, if you're comfortable with making $15 per trade when intra-day trading, then don't jump to swing trading until you're ready. The reason for this is that in swing trading you wait for a much larger $2 run for profit. This sounds great, but if you're not used to waiting for a $2 run, you will most likely break your consistency and sell your profits short because of extreme intra-day volatility.

- Finally, keep your brain in check. If you've been trading with a clear mind for several weeks straight, then don't try to trade on a day when you're struggling with a cold or dealing with emotional issues. Don't trade if you're not clear-minded. It's okay to take a day or two off. It's better to be safely on the sidelines than to find yourself down $2,500+ on a day when your head isn't screwed on straight.

Hands down, consistency either makes or breaks a trade. This is true for all trading systems. My system requires exceptionally high applications of this tool. It has hundreds of rules and procedures that must be followed to the max. Any break in consistency can easily and quickly turn a great trade into your worst nightmare.

News versus Noise

■ Learn to Resist Media Babble

As a day trader you only need to worry about news if it's going to *directly* affect the stock(s) you're intra-day trading. Other than that, don't allow the media to influence your stock picking and trading activity.

My number-one rule regarding news is very simple: if your stock is trading abnormally because of recent news releases, then stop trading it on *that day*. Sit on the sidelines and wait until the craziness settles. For the most part, news and economic reports will immediately affect trading activity on Wall Street. Your job as an independent day trader is to *not* be in a trade when the news that just hit the wire is making that stock go nuts.

Your job is to be fully aware of *when* the news hits the wire. But keep in mind, later on I will be showing you the strong swing levels; those levels typically will get broken on days of big news. I am a pro-trader so I know which levels to trade and which not to trade. This is the hardest part of my system to train you on. But for now safety is key. If you're not sure, then simply don't trade that day. Better to be safe than sorry.

■ How to Monitor News and Economic Reports

■ The most important press release on all stocks is the economic reports, particularly *quarterly earnings*. You *must* have these dates on a calendar—this is paramount. You *do not* want to be trading on the day of an earnings release. On that day your stock will most certainly have abnormal volatility. Simply trade your other stocks and wait till the next day to begin trading that stock, after the market has responded to the earnings report. Don't try to predict how Wall Street will respond to the numbers. A stock like LNKD can fluctuate 30+ dollars in 60 seconds after earnings is released, breaking all intra-day support/resistance levels without any retracement. You don't want to be part of that parabolic climb or drop.

■ Keep in mind that earnings release dates change several times leading up to the original date. Typically they're pushed out rather than bumped up. Keep rechecking.

■ How to find this data is simple and free. Simply go to Yahoo Finance. Click "News," then click the "U.S Earnings" tab, and type in your stock symbols. This will give you the next date your stock will be releasing its quarterly earnings statements. Mark your calendar and plan around that date.

■ There are several other news releases that can affect your stock during intra-day trading, including:

  ■ Fed interest rate cuts/hikes

  ■ Core product issues

  ■ Merger talks

  ■ Class action lawsuits

  ■ Bankruptcy announcements

- Employee strike threats

- CEO resignations

- Governmental interventions

- Chief competitor advancements

■ The news examples above can be found by keeping the CNBC Business News Channel on all day while you trade. Especially watch when there's a countdown clock on the bottom right-hand side of the CNBC screen.

■ You should always run a quick news search on each of your stocks, every morning before trading.

In general, if the news isn't that important to your stock, then your volume on that morning's trades will be normal and the MSNBC talking-heads will not be discussing it.

Here's a great example of news that *will* affect your stock when it gets announced in real time. Let's say the GM CEO reports that they plan to start producing all-electric cars next year. This would not be a great day for TSLA. You would want to exit immediately, either at a profit or a stop-loss. The last thing you'd want to be in that situation is a deer-in-the-headlights trader, doing nothing, freezing up. And you wouldn't want to trade that stock again until *Wall Street, not the news*, decided what to do about it. The point is you must know your stock very well, and know which news is only noise and which news can and will affect the current day's stock prices.

When It Comes to Averaging Down, Amateurs Beware!

■ It's Not Based on Real Price Levels

Here's a quick explanation of the difference between tier-trading and averaging down: the latter means you're adding to your position every time the price drops or rises in exact amounts, like 50 cents or $2. There's no emphasis as to real price levels. You're averaging into a position at nominal values that are not formed on any chart.

On the other hand, *tier-trading* is based on knowing that your first entry is one of several supports/resistances, and if the price runs against you and you choose to add to your position, the next entry will be based on a *real* level that has been formed on the chart. In later sections I revisit the tier-trading aspect of my system.

There's nothing scarier than being an amateur trader holding a 1,000+ share trade of a $100+ stock and your price is dropping precipitously. The reason why you're trading over 1,000 shares is most likely because of a reckless averaging-down strategy. You may have wisely begun your position with 100 shares off a *real* level (or not), but you quickly started adding more shares as the stock price moved against you. Since you've had no real plan, your averaging-down strategy has become reckless gambling.

In most cases, an amateur will continue averaging down until he runs out of buying power. He is basically going for broke—and this is the gambling mentality.

You may consider yourself no longer an amateur, but you can still get into this nightmare. When I was trading in Manhattan on professional trading floors, I saw pro-traders do this. Back when still getting schooled by Wall Street, I did plenty of this myself. It certainly is an amateur way of trading. So, why do advanced traders do it?

Because they're reentering at price levels simply to accumulate more shares, and not at *real* price levels. Later I show you what I mean by this, with examples of what I call "tier-trading" a position. There's a huge difference between averaging down and what I do, as you will see.

How can an amateur avoid this hellish scenario? For starters he needs to have a strict plan of execution and he must have it *prior* to every trade he enters. I know I do.

■ How to Avoid Recklessly Averaging Down

- Know all your lower/higher support/resistance levels at all times, and know them *prior* to entering your position in the first place.

- Do not add to your position if you're not clear on your price levels.

- Do not add to your position if you're trading on emotion.

- Do not add to your position if you're using margin and in a swing. If you do so, then be prepared to close out the margin portion of your position at close. Do not hold margin overnight on swings— and *never hold* an intra-day position overnight.

- You should always have a budget going into every trade, especially if it's a swing trade and you plan to hold overnight. Having a clear budget helps you make wiser decisions as to what price levels are best to tier into; anything else is reckless averaging down.

- Receive formal training so that you know exactly what levels to trade. Any other way is guesswork.

What Stocks to Trade and Why

■ I've Already Selected Them for You

Selecting stocks to day trade is one of the easiest tasks you'll encounter while trading my system. The act of actually trading them for consistent profits is the real challenge!

I've devised a stock-selection criterion system for you. This system greatly reduces a lot of guesswork in choosing the right stock to trade, and when you trade these stocks you'll have a better chance at profiting consistently.

You may already have a few stocks that you're accustomed to trading. You may have been successful at trading them in the past, but they must pass my selection process. If they *don't* pass, then you will have let them go. If you're emotionally attached to your stock(s), it will inevitably hurt you in the long run. If you have been trading a loser simply because you are trying to recapture your previous losses, then just let it go—move on.

Before we get into the actual criterion list, I want to make these two points: First, this system *does not* foretell whether the stock is going to gain or lose value in the near future. It focuses more on the consistency of the stock price's intra-day and swing fluctuations. This means that your stock should be highly predictable on how it trades. We are day traders, not investors; therefore we don't focus on what the stock will be doing next week or next month. We simply need to know how it will be trading today.

Second, your stock may be great to trade today, but it can quickly lose one of the primary criterion factors and not be worthy of your stock watch list tomorrow. For instance, when the *price drops below $100 it will simply not work with my system*. Therefore, you must monitor and research each stock every day, and become highly familiar with their news, price levels, chart patterns, and how pre-market trades. The more you trade your stock, the more this will become automatic for you.

The best advice I can give you here is to *never* become emotionally attached to your stock(s). If the stock doesn't pass the criterion-selection process, then *let it go*. Move on to better stocks that offer greater intra-day trading opportunities.

■ Learn My Stock-Selection Criterion System

Following is a list of each mandatory stock-selection criterion factor. If your stock doesn't pass *one* of these listed criteria, then you must *not* add it to your stock watch list.

■ The average daily volume (calculated over the past 12 months) must be at least 1 million shares traded daily.

There are several reasons why the daily average volume is the primary factor in my stock-selection process. The first is *liquidity*. Your stock must have sufficient intra-day trading volume. Any stock that is trading under 1 million shares per day can be easily manipulated by market makers (MMs), and they usually trade very slowly. Think about it this way: do you really want to be trading a stock that Wall Street obviously wants nothing to do with (low volume = low interest in the company)? A low-volume-traded stock simply means it's not worth trading. If you think you know something that Wall Street hasn't caught wind of, then you're setting yourself up for a major fall. Again, we are not investors, we are day traders.

We aren't trading on news or future earnings growth. We are trading on the intra-day price swings. You need high volume in order to make several roundtrip trades per day.

Second, the *differences between the bid and ask prices* become more narrow when the volume is above 1 million shares per day. Low-volume stocks usually have huge gaps between the bid and ask prices. You don't want *more than a penny gap*. Some $100+ stocks will have larger bid/ask spreads, depending on the *time of day*. If the bid price is $135.25, then the ask price should be $135.26. This single factor will make more sense once you begin trading live.

■ The stock price must be between $100 and $250.

For now all you need to know is that the stocks in this price range are the most highly traded stocks on Wall Street, but also have the largest volatility. We love volatility!

Also consider that most stocks priced over $100 will already exemplify virtually all the fundamental criteria that make up a great company. They will have consistent volumes, consistent liquidity, and most importantly, are consistently traded by Wall Street.

Later you will realize that these stocks happen to be the most traded by black-box (high-frequency trading systems). This normally isn't good for investors but is great for my system because the algorithms built into the software that runs it are relatively easy for seeing the patterns, the price levels. I show you the framework later as to how I find and trade those price levels.

In a nutshell, stocks in the price range are the best to trade when using my system, which is a countertrend trading methodology.

"Why not priced *over* $250?" Quite simply, because they are too expensive at that point and take up too much of your capital. They also start to have huge bid/ask gaps, and they will mostly stock-split soon, so there's no sense in trading them anymore.

■ The average intraday price swings must be sufficient to trade (as evidenced by chart analysis).

In Figure L13.1 there is a sample chart that would be sufficient to trade. You want a chart pattern that is consistently fluctuating intra-day. Your stock should be moving at least 15 cents every

BIDU 5 minute chart

FIGURE L13.1 Five-Minute Chart Over Three Days

10 seconds to 5 minutes. In the chart the price range over a few days remains in a tight trading range between $215 and $220.

Over time you will begin to see and understand these ideal chart patterns. For now, simply look for chart patterns that complement the one in Figure L13.1.

■ There must be no stocks affected by *frequent* government regulations.

If the stock/company is regularly affected by government regulations and/or approvals—*do not trade it*. Great examples of stocks that usually are very risky to trade are biotech stocks and military defense stocks. Obviously, recent trading of banks has not been great due to frequent government regulations and low interest rates. Therefore, you shouldn't be currently trading them. But, traditionally biotech and military defense stocks tend to move over 50 percent in one single day when the news hits the wire (good or bad news), whether it be the FDA declining approval or approving a new drug, or the Defense Department cutting the future border control budget affecting several companies that produce products involving terrorist detection.

You never want to deal with this kind of volatility and uncertainty. Don't ever try to predict how Wall Street will respond to this news. Simply avoid these stocks and any other stocks that find themselves in the national-economic spotlight of uncertainty. There are plenty of stocks out there that are not facing a complete meltdown.

- There must be no current news headlines that directly affect the stock.

    Similar to the previous criterion, this factor involves outside influences. If your stock is constantly in the news headlines due to a major economic issue taking place, then don't trade it. Wait it out.

    Stocks that are constantly affected by the news tend to be highly volatile, and they tend to have very unpredictable charting patterns. You're supposed to be avoiding the noise. You can very easily get sidetracked and stumped by the news that's currently affecting your stock intra-day.

    If you notice that your stock is trading directly on breaking news, then sit on the sidelines and wait. Trade your other stocks *not* affected by the news until the dust settles.

- There must be no chance, in the near future, that the company will file for bankruptcy.

    This final criterion is very obvious, but you'd be surprised how many amateurs try to trade a stock facing bankruptcy. Usually the stock price is less than $100 on companies facing bankruptcy (so you should *not* be trading it anyway), but some are still in the process of falling from high price levels.

    The problem with companies facing the possibility of bankruptcy is that the news comes out when you least expect it. And you never know the real details of the bankruptcy until it's too late. Again, you don't want to be trading a stock that has the possibility of losing over 50 percent of its value in one single day.

If you're in my training program, you'll be able to watch the 8 to 10 stocks that I trade consistently every day. Watching my stocks and my levels in real time every day is the best way to speed up your learning process. Once you master my system, you can then add your own stocks and become more independent.

Picking the Right Online Broker

■ Pay-per-Share versus Pay-per-Trade Brokers

There are pay-per-trade brokers and there are pay-per-share brokers. The main difference boils down to how much is your expense, or the commission you pay, *per trade*.

If you're a pro day trader, meaning you execute several roundtrip trades each day, then you need to have a low commission structure. I define *low* as paying *between 40 cents and $1.00 per trade when trading in 100-share blocks*.

Experience has shown me that most amateur day traders don't use pay-per-share brokers and they don't trade consistently in 100-share blocks. Much of the reason is that the traditional online brokerage industry, which is all about pay-per-trade brokers, maneuvers to retain amateur loyalty.

Here's a big secret that the pay-per-trade brokers don't want beginners to learn of. There are online brokers who charge as little as $.004 cents *per share* (pay-per-share). That amounts to about 40 cents per trade when trading in 100-share blocks. To the amateur who trades through a pay-per-trade broker and pays $5 to $10 *per trade*, no matter how many shares are purchased, to hear about that is a shocker—and good news. The few cents you read about above is no misprint.

"What's the catch?" amateurs ask me. "How come I never heard of pay-per-share online brokers?" And then they want to know: "Why only purchase 100 shares per trade?" Those are understandable questions. The answers may be surprising.

First, when you trade through a pay-per-share broker, there's no scam or catch at all. It's all about becoming more professional. If you plan on evolving to a "pattern day trader," which means you plan to make several intra-day roundtrip trades, then you need a pay-per-share broker.

There is one condition that I suppose you could call a catch, but it's really a form of promotion: when you begin to advance as a day trader, which naturally involves pay-per-share, you'll find yourself becoming more and more regulated by the SEC. As I mentioned before, you need a minimum of 25K and the balance of your account cannot fall below that when intra-day trading stocks. If it does drop below that amount, you get hit with an "equity call." That means that you can't trade on margin until you deposit enough funds to return your balance up to 25K.

If you're turned off by this financial requirement, then most likely you're not financially ready for professional day trading. Consider these facts: if you want to day trade for a living, then you need to make several intra-day trades without getting constantly hit in the wallet by those whopping pay-per-trade commissions. And you need at east 25K to make any real money.

I've mentioned that the pay-per-trade brokers maneuver to keep amateurs with them. One of the ways they do this is by pairing with popular training outfits that sign up huge groups of beginners. These day trading seminars and training programs usually don't tell you about pay-per-share firms, because they contract with pay-per-trade brokers. They sign you up and train you on their trading platforms during the training program. This enables such pay-per-trade brokers to profit off your trading activity. When I ponder that, the word *racket* comes to mind.

Also, pay-per-share firms don't advertise in primetime commercials. You only hear about them from experienced people like me. Because they seek only serious day traders, they prefer to keep a low profile.

Next question: Why just 100 shares per trade? The answer is simple: you're better safe than sorry. You're an amateur and you need to learn how to day trade in a cautiously low-risk environment. When trading in 100-share blocks, you're not going to overexpose yourself to market uncertainty.

Think about it. If you're trading 1,000 shares of a stock and it drops $2 intra-day, then you're in the red $2,000. Can you handle that kind of a scare? Can you handle that several times a day? If you only purchase 100 shares, however, then you're only potentially in the red by a measly $200. That's more psychologically manageable, especially for a beginner. Very few amateurs can stay consistently profitable when day trading in 1,000+ share blocks.

So how can amateurs start trading like the pros?

Most pro-traders' approach to day trading involves the following:

- Making many intra-day trades and swing trades

- Taking relatively small profits on each intra-day and swing trade

- Exiting losing trades quickly (at a predetermined price level), without emotion

- Minimizing commission costs

Most pro-traders place at least 50 trades per day (that's 25 roundtrip trades or more). They do both intra-day and swing trades. In that multiple-trade scenario, you don't need to purchase large share blocks. This is why most pro-traders find it safer and cheaper to place their trades in 100-share blocks, typically never accumulating more than 500 shares on a single position.

Another advantage to 100-share blocks is that orders get filled (buying and selling) much faster. Look at any Level 2 quote chart and you'll see all the streaming orders being placed. You'll note that most filled orders are between 100 and 500 shares at a time (as illustrated in the Level 2 quote chart in Figure L14.1).

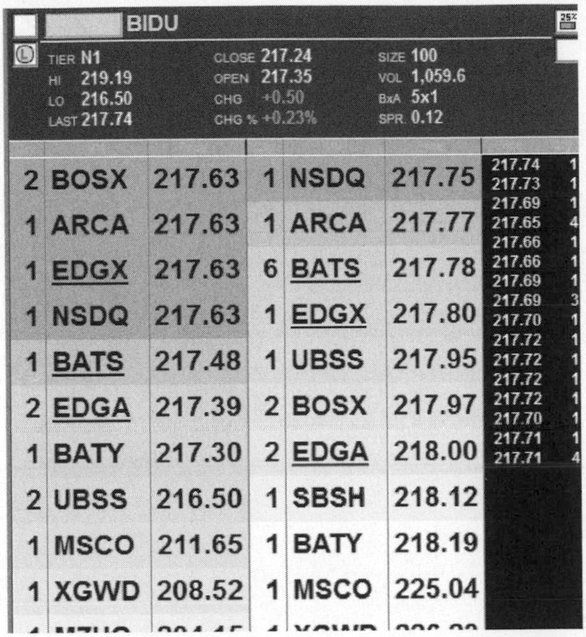

FIGURE L14.1 Streaming Level 2 Quote Chart from Lightspeed Trading Platform

Taking small profits and small manageable losses is the key to remaining consistent all day. We pros look for quick 15-cent moves in the stock price on intra-day trades, so the pay-per-share commission structure is critical. Since most of the time we're trading in 100-share blocks, we chance to profit $15 on each trade. We normally don't stay in a trade over 15 minutes, and usually we're simultaneously trading at least three other stocks. So those *small profits* add up considerably.

There are several other features and benefits that pay-per-share trading firms offer. Other than low commission structures, the largest benefit to trading through pay-per-share brokers is *direct access trading platforms*. Direct access means that when you place a trade, it's not going through a middleman broker. You are purchasing directly from the market. You can purchase at the real *ask* price immediately. Also, direct access trading platforms offer FASTKEY order execution capabilities. This means you can use your keyboard buttons to execute orders. You will soon find out how awesome that is.

I always use a pay-per-share trading platform and commission structure. You will be using a demo trading platform during my program that has direct access Level 2 data feeds, meaning real-time demo trading.

"What if I only want to swing trade for $1.50 to $2.00 profits?" You can keep you current pay-per-trade broker and pay $9.99 per trade and still net decent profits. But why pay more in fees than you have to? And there are other factors to consider, such as the direct access of your current bid/ask prices. You will soon learn how important pre-market data is. Many brokers don't offer trading during pre-market.

## PART II

DAY TRADER JOSH'S INTRA-DAY TRADING METHODOLOGY

Note: This section is divided into four parts that must be read in the order presented. To maximize your understanding of my system, do not skip ahead at any time.

Chapter 1: Basic Procedure

- Picking stocks priced from $100 to $250

- Taking consistent profits of 15 cents per 100 shares

- Practice with stop-loss safeguards: max loss $3

Chapter 2: *Prior* Price Levels and Newly Forming Intra-Day Levels

- General framework to intra-day strategy
- Basic charting: using one-minute candlesticks
- The prior price levels: three definite S/R levels
- Basic rules and procedures for acquiring daily price levels
- Logging levels on whiteboard prior to opening bell
- Recognizing newly forming intra-day support/resistance

Chapter 3: Intra-Day Golden Rules: Entry/Exit Setups

- Golden Rules for intra-day trading: application
- Three-tier max strategy: 100-share block trades
- Fifteen-cent max static profits
- Framework: entry and exit strategy step-by-step procedures and guidelines
- Intra-day trading risk: strategy stop-loss

Chapter 4: The Mechanics of FASTKEY Order Execution

- Using your keyboard keys for rapid order execution
- Placing orders directly from Level 2 quote chart (direct access)
- Executing real-time trades (manual limit orders)
- Back-testing: both real-time and end-of-day trades

## CHAPTER 1

Basic Procedure

Pick stocks priced between $100 and $250.

Stocks in the $100 to $250 range are the best stocks to trade with my system. These are the stocks that react the best to my intra-day enter/exit strategy. They tend to move very fast, and they offer more intra-day trade setups. Also they only require 100-share block trades, thus keeping your commissions fees lower.

For instance, if you're trading a lower priced stock—let's say in the $10–$30 range—in order to make any money you have to purchase 500 shares on each trade. When you're trading through a pay-per-share broker, this means you're paying 500 percent more in commissions on each trade.

Even stocks priced at $90 tend to be slow movers and will not react properly to my system. So keep this in mind from now on: if you're accustomed to trading stocks priced *under $100*, you *cannot* trade them with my system. Soon you'll understand why.

■ The Best Stocks to Trade with My System

The first point I want to make is that the stocks you pick now will be traded with *both* intra-day and swing systems. Most S&P 500 stocks priced $100–$250 will be sufficient to trade my system. Most will be *blue chip* stocks—these are Wall Street's stocks!

Another very important criterion is that the company should have experienced a couple of earnings release dates and should have always remained above $100. This proves their consistency. Here's a precise rule to follow:

> The stock must have had at least two consecutive earnings releases and remained above $100 for an entire six-month period.

If your stock does fall below $100, then you immediately stop trading it and wait until the next earnings release until you start trading it again. A great example is BIDU. As you can see in the chart in Figure 1.1, it dropped below $100 and then shot back after earnings, where it remained above $100. Then I started trading it again.

Picking stocks should *not* feel like pulling teeth. It should *not* be scary guesswork. My system of trading requires that you remain with the same stocks for an extended period—perhaps your entire day trading career. Some stocks, like IBM, have been trading above $100 for more than five years straight and have never been above $250. For those reasons, IBM is one of the most consistently traded stocks in my trading room and on Wall Street.

The more familiar you become with your stock(s), the better you'll get at applying my trading method, particularly the "rhythm factor." You need to be in perfect rhythm with your stock. You must get

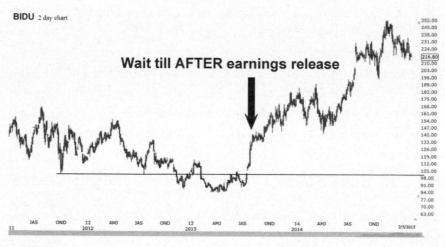

FIGURE 1.1   BIDU 2-Day Chart

to know its patterns—the speed of its price movements, or its lack of speed.

For instance, I'm currently trading GS and TSLA. I can guarantee that TSLA moves at least three times faster than GS, and that at earnings releases, TSLA will gap up/down three times as much—even when their price levels are not very different.

In this manual you'll be viewing several charts with $100+ stocks. These stocks are great examples of what works best with my system. The main point I want to have resonate with you is that once you find your stock, you stick with it every day for at least three months.

Why? Every three months, you have earnings release dates. Your stock may fall below $100 after earnings is announced and Wall Street sells off shares; or just the opposite happens—it rises well above $250 and can't be traded anymore. Two great examples of stock over $250 are AAPL and AMZN. (I'm referring of course to AAPL prior to the 7:1 split in 2014.) I was trading AMZN and APPL very consistently until they each started climbing above $250. They started moving much faster than I was accustomed to, and most importantly, they ate up way too much of my capital buying power. Also, the spread between bid/ask was ridiculous! In some cases the spread was as much as $1 during regular market hours.

Later I show that, while the bid/ask spread is not so important with regard to swing entries, for intra-day entries it's critical; the spreads can't be that far apart. The reason for this is when you're trading intra-day, a spread that's too wide will make you miss your trades—that applies to both entries and exits. As I've mentioned before, ideally the spread should be only a penny, and never more than 25 cents.

If you're a greenhorn and you've just read that and you glance at a *pre-market* Level 2 chart, you will certainly see some humongous spreads between the bid/ask prices. You will see this after hours and on weekends as well. This is normal; it doesn't mean anything. The only thing you should remember for now is that when trying to determine if a stock between $100 and $250 has a tight gap (less than 25 cents) you want to make sure that the time that you watch is between 9:30 A.M. and 4:00 P.M. EST—only during market hours.

FIGURE 1.2 IBM Weekly Chart

Figure 1.2 is an example of how some stocks can consistently trade between $100 and $250 for over five years. IBM is certainly one of my most traded stocks.

There's one other major factor that helps me determine whether I should add a stock to my list or whether I should take it down. The stock must have pre-market data. You will soon learn just how important the pre-market levels are and how to use them. Many stocks, even high-priced stocks over $100, do not have pre-market data. A great example is RL. I used to trade it, but once the pre-market data stopped, I had no choice—I had to get rid of it.

BASIC PROCEDURE

Take consistent profits of 15 cents per 100-block trade.

In this next section I map the framework for how you find your intra-day setups. Once you know your entry you'll execute the order, and once you're filled you'll immediately throw a limit order for a 15-cent profit. This will be the same on every trade, no more and no less. This is critical to your long-term profitability. Consistency is key.

My system is based on taking *profits on the reversals* from intra-day trends. In fact, you can consider it *countertrend trading* both for intra-day and swing setups. When you're countertrend trading there are *always* key price levels that *retrace* when broken, particularly with our specialized stocks. My goal is to show you how to spot these levels forming in real time.

The key reason why I never seek more than 15 cents on each trade is that small reversals in price usually do not run more than 25 cents, even when I trade $100+ stocks. In other words, in order to have a higher probability of consistent profits off the intra-day reversals in price, you should never try to get more than 15 cents; 25 cents is twice as hard to achieve as taking a 15-cent profit. This will make much more sense when you start testing my system on the demo trading platform in my training program.

Also keep in mind that you'll ultimately be seeking swing trades and profiting $1.50 or more, so there's no sense in trying to achieve more than 15 cents on an intra-day quick trade.

From this point forward, you should put yourself on high alert for the ravenous mouth of the *greed factor*. And be very mindful of this: suppose you're trying to get 25 cents on *all* trades (a static limit order). You'll quickly find that half your trades will go 15 cents into the green and then retrace back into the red. Therefore, all your exit points (at a profit) should be exactly the same at 15 cents, or you may turn a profit into a loss.

■ Additional Reasons Why You Should Take Only 15 Cents on Each Trade

My system of intra-day trading depends on the general market barriers of 25 cents. Due to these barriers, it's more difficult to profit over 25 cents on each trade. There are four 25-cent barriers at any given time of day and price level. I list them in the chart in Figure 1.3.

If you're trading IBM, for instance, and it's currently priced at $154.<u>20</u>, and the price has been trending up from that price level,

```
The four 25 cent barriers:

.00
.25
.50
.75
```

FIGURE 1.3   25-Cent Barriers

then here are the next general market barriers (or general resistance when the price is increasing):

$154.<u>25</u>, first 25 cents barrier at .<u>25</u>
$154.<u>50</u>, then
$154.<u>75</u>, then
$155.00, then ...

The 25-cent general market barriers *do not* mean you trade short/long positions simply because they hit these levels—of course not. I thoroughly revisit this later. For now, understand that 15-cent profit taking is the max you will profit once you enter your intra-day trade.

> Practice with stop-loss safeguards with a max loss of $3.

I elaborate this strategy in Chapter 3. There you will learn that I *do not* use static stop-loss orders such as exiting a trade if I'm $300 in the red or if my position goes 5 percent against me—quite the opposite. I've devised an alternative method of stop-loss, and I call it *strategy stop-loss*. I offer a couple of examples below because I know you're probably scratching your head after reading that I don't have static stop-loss orders built into my system.

The most common situation where I strategy-stop-loss is at the closing bell. I do this if I'm in the red and holding *intra-day* positions. (As I've mentioned before, this doesn't apply in swing trading. With those you can hold overnight.) I also stop-loss if I need to immediately free up some capital to allocate to another stock trade that's more likely to profit that day. I use this maneuver for both intra-day and swing trades.

Other examples are: I stop-loss on the day of an earnings release. I stop-loss if devastating news hits the wire. (When I say *devastating*, I mean the entire market is blitzed. I hate to say it, but 9/11? That bad!) In other words, I only stop-loss when my risk factors are enormous or I need to quickly free up some capital.

Finally, one of my biggest reasons to strategy-stop-loss is when I find that my price levels and/or entry levels are off, or if I made a mistake.

Remember that when you use my system, you *do not* exit at a loss simply because the price runs against you. This may be hard to swallow, because in most cases the price *will* run against you. That's totally normal with my system and you need to *get used to it*. It makes no sense whatsoever to stop-loss when down a nominal value or percentage.

"Why not?" you might ask. This system will show you that if you're in the red, then you're about to hit even stronger entry levels, those levels you need to enter at. *So why would you be exiting at a loss when you should be adding to your current trade?* The answer to this question will take some time and experience to digest. Even after learning the framework here, this is by far one of the most critical reasons why you can't learn this system in its entirety on paper.

For instance, chances are you've been taught to stop-loss when down a certain amount or percentage. That's how most amateurs trade. In my training program you learn the exact opposite. I need to reprogram you, and I can't do that without coaching you, and I can't coach you on paper.

The hardest part of this system is not getting scared when in the red. You need thick skin to be a real day trader. Most traders who attempt this without formal training make the same mistake: they cut their profits early, break even, or simply stop-loss when deep in the red. On the contrary, when using my system you'll find that if you had just held a bit longer and added to your position at key levels, then it would have been a profit.

I'm sure you've had this happen: you exit a trade at a loss, and 10 minutes later or a day later the stock price reverses back to the green, but you exited already, so no dice. I can promise your fear will make this happen to you if you don't master this system. Even advanced traders in my one-year program still struggle with this psychological barrier.

Remember: this is countertrend trading. I don't expect it to make much sense right now, but I promise that later you'll understand why I don't use nominal values or percentages to determine a stop-loss exit. Think about it. If I were to stop-loss every time I got $3 in the red ($300 loss on 100 shares), then about 90 percent of all my past profitable trades would be losses instead, to date. I'm showing you, greenhorn, how to be safe instead of sorry.

And now you might ask: "So why a static $3 stop-loss right here in this lesson?" In the swing strategy part you'll learn that you should start intra-day trading positions once your intra-day setups are within $3 of your swing entry. This does not mean you simply enter a trade once you're within $3 of a swing level. It certainly isn't that easy.

My purpose is to get you used to intra-day trading while in the red as much as $3. That translates to $300 in the red when holding a 100-share position. If you don't know your swing levels yet, then you need to be prepared to exit trade once you're down $3. Simply put, I'm enforcing a *static $3 stop-loss rule* here for the purpose of *training only*.

I *cannot* stress this enough right now: if I'm in the red, I *do not* intra-day trade and simply take $300 losses. Of course not—this is strictly for learning purposes. Until you master the swing levels, you need to learn to stop-loss on your intra-day trades. I can almost guarantee you that you will make a gazillion mistakes on picking the correct intra-day levels to trade. Therefore, the $3 stop-loss is a safety measure for beginners to this system.

In the next part I show you a very specific trading strategy that's enforced with specific rules and procedures that you need to know when attempting intra-day trading with this system. You'll inevitably make classic mistakes, and that's why I just showed you the $300 max stop-loss safeguard.

## CHAPTER 2

Prior Price Levels and Newly Forming Intra-Day Levels

In this chapter we discuss the general framework of my intra-day strategy.

I've established that the framework of my intra-day method is based on *countertrend reversal*. To reiterate, this is about waiting on the sidelines for a price trend to hit either support or resistance levels. Whatever direction it moves in doesn't matter. Either way, you have a trade. If the price travels *up* and breaks resistance levels, then you'll have a *short* position to trade. If the price travels *down* and breaks support levels, then you'll have a *long* position to trade.

If you're reading about my system for the first time, you may be feeling puzzled right now. What I'm saying is most likely exactly the opposite of what you're accustomed to. Allow me to clarify.

My system is based on a principle that flies in the face of momentum/trend trading, which is the conventional way to trade. Instead of the usual predicting or guessing as to how far Wall Street will continue a price run, I patiently wait for that price run to hit overbought or oversold price levels, and that's where I make my money.

"What price levels?" you might ask. The answers are provided in this section. I refer to them as *prior levels*, which means the levels we establish *before* the market has opened that day.

Let's recap the basic elements of intra-day trading in my system:

- I only take 15 cents on intra-day setups.

- I max my tiers to *three prior* price levels, meaning 300 shares max.

- I enter the trade 50 cents past my intraday support/resistance.

- The *only* newly formed intra-day levels I trade are the highs/lows of the day.

- I *never* hold an intraday trade overnight.

I'll elaborate on the three prior price levels in a moment. First, here are some chart-reading pointers.

For *basic* charting, use one-minute candlesticks.

My intra-day trading method is based on *price action*. The *one-minute* candlestick chart offers the most transparency on price movements, making it my primary time frame for determining intra-day support and resistance levels. The only technical indicator I add to the chart is the *volume bar*. Each candlestick has a corresponding volume bar. I use these two essentials exclusively. All other indicators simply don't have any relevance, not in such short time frames.

Most indicators, such as Bollinger bands, Fibonacci lines, and MACD, and so on, are only used in investing, and in my opinion, they're useless even then.

Note: I strongly suggest that you purchase at least two *27-inch+ LCD screens*. If you don't, you'll find that if you can't view the *entire* trading session on your screen from 8 A.M. to 4 P.M., then you'll have a hard time viewing and recognizing *previous* intra-day support/resistance levels. In other words, you need to be able to see each one-minute candlestick across the screen for the entire day, and each candlestick has to be clearly definable/visible.

Figure 2.1 is an example of a one-minute candlestick chart.

FIGURE 2.1 One-Minute Candlesticks

■ The Basics of One-Minute Candlestick Chart Reading

As shown in Figure 2.2:

- The *wick* of the candlestick shows both the high and low price in that time frame.

- The *body* of the candlestick can also show the high/low price.

  Example: The 12:38 candlestick has a high (#1) of 157.67 and a low (#2) of 157.54. Notice how in this case it's the wick that determines the H/L price.

  Example: The 12:40 candlestick has a high (#3) of 157.71 and a low (#4) of 157.57. Notice how the high price is part of the body, and the low is part of wick.

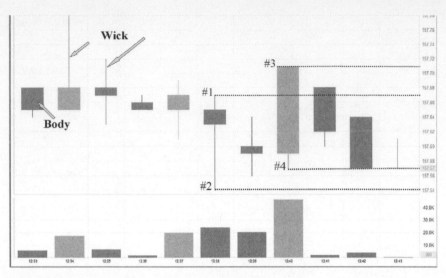

FIGURE 2.2 One-Minute Candlestick Chart

Please note: the color of a candlestick *does not* matter with my system. And the high or low price can be part of the *wick* and/or *body*. All that matters is that you know the *high/low* of *each* one-minute candlestick.

> In the *prior* price levels, there are three *definite* support/resistance levels.

Here you will learn the basic structure of my intra-day setup procedure. It starts before the bell rings each morning with a gathering from *three prior price ranges*. I refer to those ranges as *prior* because they always exist *before* 9:30 A.M. EST.

Your pre-market trading session will always have a high and a low price, your previous day will always have a high and a low price, and on your daily charts you will always have several highs and lows. Each new trading session begins at 8:00 A.M. (pre-market) and then, at 9:30 A.M., the bell rings for the regular market trading hours.

When the 9:30 bell rings, you are guaranteed to *always* have *three* previous *support levels* and *resistance levels* from which to *initially* trade. As both support and resistance, those levels are very strong and can be traded every day on all your stocks. It's critical that you properly log them. Here's how.

Those three *prior* support/resistance levels come from these definite price levels:

1. Pre-market high/low
2. Previous day high/low
3. Daily high/low

1. Pre-Market High/Low

Pre-market trading should be observed in real time. Most direct access platforms have this capability, and on most it starts at 6:00 A.M.

Most active orders start at 8:00 A.M., so I use 8:00 to begin logging price range. Our stocks priced over $100 are traded in pre-market. The volume will be much lower than regular hours, but regardless, the orders placed then are important and relevant. You'll have a lowest pre-market price and also a highest price.

Your job is to wait till the bell rings, and then determine exactly what the high/low pre-market levels are. You will *not* know for certain until 9:29:59 A.M. Typically, they're forming every second, right up to the opening bell. Once the bell rings at 9:30 A.M., the market has its first definable trading range of the day. The range is from 8:00 to 9:30 A.M. You have a high and a low there.

The pre-market range is your most *current,* which means the high and low prices during pre-market trading are your most relevant levels. At this point you can see how important it is to log your pre-market data. Here's how.

Your chart needs to be set to one-minute candles to make 6:00 A.M. viewable. You want to see back to 6:00 A.M. just in case price levels do hit. It's very rare that your high/low during pre-market trading will hit between 6:00 and 8:00 A.M., but you do need to be aware. If it's a heavy volume morning for your stock, then you must be on pre-market high alert. Other than that, you only use the 8:00–9:29 A.M. range.

Here's what to look for. The price levels will appear as dots on the screen. Use your crosshair(s) to determine what exactly are the price levels at each dot on the chart. The highest price filled during pre-market trading is your *resistance* level and the lowest price filled is your *support* level.

Figure 2.3 shows the entire *pre-market trading range* from 8:00 to 9:30 A.M. The resistance (high) is 157.13 and the support (low) is 156.10.

2. Previous Day High/Low

This is the easiest high/low to acquire. You simply take the high price and low price of the previous day's candlestick. Make sure that you're not including the pre-market and aftermarket prices. They must be the high and low prices between 9:30 A.M. and 4:00 P.M. (see Figure 2.4).

I show you in later sections how to trade earnings. Only then do the aftermarket and pre-market high/low prices matter.

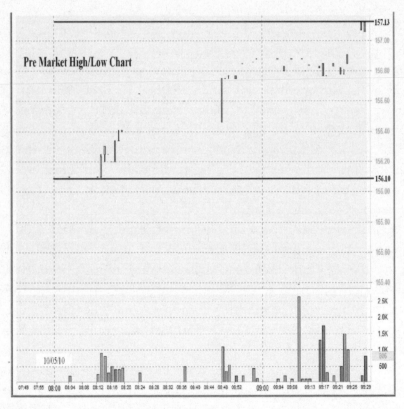

FIGURE 2.3   Pre-Market Trading Range

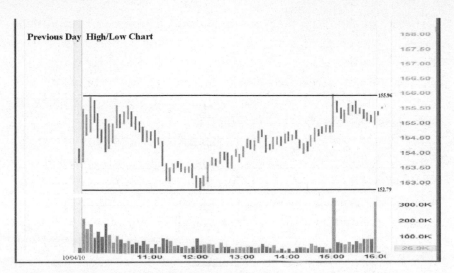

FIGURE 2.4 Previous Day High/Low Chart

3. Daily High/Low (Resistance/Support)

The daily high/low levels are the most important levels of my system and the most important levels traded in high volume by Wall Street. As you will discover, those levels are the basis of my *fusion* of both intra-day and swing setups.

Besides their significance, the daily price levels are also the most complex to find and trade. Therefore, they take far more explaining than pre-market high/low levels and previous day high/low levels.

When you master the daily price levels, you're one step closer to trading the same levels that Wall Street recognizes. Again and again you're going to see how well the price movements pivot at or near those levels and with how much consistency. Only Wall Street can form them. As the small retail pro-traders, our job is to thoroughly know them. It's critical to update them every day.

You will find that those levels are not so hard to gather. Keeping them up to date is the challenge. This takes a big dose of due diligence every single morning before the bell rings. Here I will show you several techniques for gathering and displaying those price levels.

(Later, in the chapter on swing trading, I utilize the same daily levels. However, their function in swing trading is more complicated than in intra-day setups. I'm teaching you the intra-day setups first because the daily levels are easier to learn when you're only intra-day trading. Once you get to the swing trading, I add tougher scenarios and rules. For now we're just taking baby steps.)

I said that gathering the daily levels isn't hard, but it can be intricate. It does require focus and skill. Remember, this book is only the framework. I know I'm being redundant, but it can't be said enough: to learn this you need to be coached and hands-on.

I keep mentioning price levels. From this point on you will begin to understand just how much my system depends on those levels more than any other chart indicator. Wall Street day traders use price levels. They do *not* use the *leading indicators* that most nonprofessional trading platforms boast, such as MACD lines, Bollinger bands, R%, and so on.

> The single most important factor that dictates a price reversal is the price level itself.

I know that sounds obvious but a lot of my readers may have two or more chart indicators, and they depend a lot more on those darting squiggle lines than on the price levels themselves. This is true because most trading programs teach their trainees to do that. They know that the greenhorns relate to those lines with a false sense of security, thinking they need them to help them decide.

Figure 2.5 is a perfect example of way too much information. It confuses and makes real-time decisions much harder, especially the exacting of the right price levels for entering into a trade. This may impress a beginner, but it's actually a screenshot from one of my greenhorns who was trading with my system along with some junk that he learned at a two-hour seminar. He lost a lot of money before he dumped the junk and started to trust my system.

For now, just remember this: the price levels on a daily chart are the most important indicator for price reversals that you'll ever use when trading equities. Figure 2.6 is a simple daily candlestick chart. At first glance it has no definable pattern or support/resistance

FIGURE 2.5 Too Much Information

DAILY CHART: LNKD

FIGURE 2.6 Daily Chart: LNKD

price levels. Later I show you this chart again with the major price levels and no other indicator.

Right now you might ask me: "Why are daily price levels so important?" The stock market began with *real* price levels, and the stock market still uses *real* price levels for bid/ask. So why use anything else? When determining their entry/exit orders, most highly leveraged Wall Street trading firms *only* use black-box high-frequency software that combines price levels with volume. (Yes, volume is an indicator, the only other one that's worthwhile, but novices rarely use it properly. I have a hard time reading volume. I return to that later on.)

Wall Street uses daily price levels, not so-called leading indicators, because price levels are the most transparent real-time gauges for trades. You're going to find that most leading indicators *lag*, meaning they only represent *what's happened* but not *what will happen next*—not with any high degree of certainty. Three lines cross-secting and converging on a chart does *not* mean you buy or sell at that junction, so why clog up your screen with those bogus bells and whistles? I get that it looks cool, like fireworks going off, but you're setting yourself up for failure. Just use real price levels. That's all we use.

Finding and logging daily high/low price levels involves basic chart analysis. You set your chart settings to view *daily* candlesticks. When you read the rules that dictate daily levels, you may think they're very simplistic. That's because here I just give you the framework. Finding the daily levels is one thing. Learning how to trade them is something else entirely.

> You must learn the basic rules and procedures for acquiring *daily level*.

You set your chart to a candlestick pattern. You must be able to view back as far as 10-plus years. But you start with the most current, most recently formed daily levels. You log all the levels, even if they're $50-plus off the current price.

You have two basic price levels: your daily lows (supports) and your daily highs (resistance). To find them on the *daily chart*, you start with these procedures:

- To find the *daily lows*, look at the most current day on the candlestick chart and start scanning to its left until you find the first candle that has *at least four higher* candlesticks to its *left and right*, meaning the price level has held for at least nine trading sessions.

Note: This will typically resemble a "V" shape.

- To find the *daily highs*, look at the most current day on the candlestick chart and start scanning to its left until you find the first candle that has *at least four lower* candlesticks to its *left and right*, meaning the price level has held for at least nine trading sessions.

Note: This will typically resemble a "pyramid" shape.

Figure 2.7 is a basic illustration of a sample *daily level* with established highs and lows.

Note that each price level has at least *four candlesticks* on each side of the daily price level. This means the price held for *at least nine days straight* without breaking that level.

Once you start gathering the proper price levels, you'll find that there are several daily price levels that match this basic criterion.

FIGURE 2.7   Daily Level with Highs and Lows

Here are some rules that will help you eliminate several weaker daily levels:

- Each daily level should be *$1.00 or more* than the other.

- If you have more than one daily price level within $1.00 of each other, then you choose the lowest/highest.

Figure 2.8 illustrates this process.

In this case you simply disregard the 234.83 daily price level and log the 235.37 instead. Note that at one point in time you would have been using the 234.83 price level, but once the 235.37 was a confirmed level, four candlesticks later, on 01/29, it trumped the previous 234.83 daily level. You will understand this better later. For now just get familiar with the chart and get used to looking at candlesticks (price levels).

FIGURE 2.8 Daily Level Process

Another rule is to disregard levels over one year (52 weeks). *Unless*:

- The price level *was or is an all-time high/low.*

- And/or it has *over 30 days* to its left and right.

- Or it's *over 2 years.* Then it must be *more than* $5.00 off other daily levels.

Figure 2.9 illustrates when daily levels are *over a year* but still relevant. And it also shows dates that drop off because they are too weak.

I'm writing this on February 19, 2015. In order for the price levels to be relevant today, the daily levels *before* February 29, 2014, would have to have at least 30 consecutive days on each side of the level holding below/above.

Note that the 257.56 daily price level on September 11, 2013, has at least 30 days holding consecutively on *both* sides. At that time it

DAILY CHART: LNKD

FIGURE 2.9 Daily Levels Over a Year

was an all-time high. Now look just to the right. You have the 255.84 daily price level on September 26, 2013. It's more than $1 off the 257.56 level but you can't use it anymore, because it doesn't hold for 30 days to the left.

The main reason for this critical rule is to insure that if your price level is old, then it had better be an extremely strong level if it's going to be relevant today. Levels that meet the criterion—over a year old and holding for more than 30 days—remain relevant in today's trading, especially when the current price is approaching them.

Of equal importance is the *gap* rule. Figure 2.10 shows how a gap of $10 or more overnight means you do not need to have the candle to the left higher/lower for confirmation on support/resistance.

Chances are that when this happens, it's due to a major price run after an earnings release date. You will typically see this pattern every three months on the daily charts. The gap rule applies quite often.

TSLA DAILY CHART

FIGURE 2.10   Gap Rule

Note that the *high* of the February 24, 2014, candlestick is 218.36, and dually note that the *low* of the February 25, 2014, candlestick is 228.45. The overnight gap is more than $10. In this case, the daily price level is the low of 228.45. And, the high of 218.36 would also be a daily *high* level.

The rules I just mapped out on gathering daily price levels are about 90 percent of what you need. You also need awareness of the remaining 10 percent, and that's where things can get tricky. I can't possibly span all the rules that apply to all the circumstances you're going to encounter—not because it can't be written down here, but because certain stocks and certain situations demand adjustments to the rules and procedures.

For instance, certain stocks do not need exactly 30 days holding. And with some stocks you need your levels at least $2 apart as opposed to the standard $1. These are gray areas that emerge from time to time, especially during earnings season, and that can be a time of turmoil and error if you don't know this system entirely.

Different rules for different stocks: this is why training on any particular stock takes weeks, if not months, to fully grasp on my system. In *The Truth About Day Trading Stocks*, I discuss the *rhythm factor*. To reiterate, each stock has its own unique rhythm. If you just apply the framework I sketch here to all stocks priced $100–$250, then you're not in sync with your stock. I elaborate this crucial point later.

This price-oriented day trading system can only be learned from practice and application in real-time. The wise thing to do is to get formal training on how to handle gray areas and other stumbling blocks.

■ Get Your Daily Price Levels Logged and Organized

Once you have your daily levels logged, you can begin to *consider* trading them. I say that you should only *consider* because you *don't* trade these levels simply because they're hitting. If you do that, I promise you will lose all your money. There is a process, and there are procedures to follow, and the system will tell you the exact price level you should enter at, if and only if you have it mastered. I will get to this shortly.

■ What to Do After You Have Your List of Daily High Price Levels and Daily Low Price Levels

I'll begin with a critical rule. To determine what daily levels to use for *today's trading*, *only* include figures *within $10* of pre-market trading (the high and low price of pre-market). For example, if a stock is trading near $231 in pre-market trading hours, then pick only *daily* low/high levels that are approximately within $10 above or below $231. This *does not* mean that if the stock price runs for more than $10, you *do not* use higher/lower levels. This procedure pertains to what I refer to as my *whiteboard logs*.

What is a whiteboard log? It's a simple drawing board for logging price levels in huge writing with erasable markers. I learned to do this while trading near Wall Street on equity trading floors. Many of the pros were doing this at their trade stations. The simple reason why is to be able to see the important price levels at a quick glance and from far away if not sitting. I have several on my walls surrounding my trade station.

What's on the whiteboards? They each document the levels that pertain to that particular day's trading on each stock I'm trading. They always have the *prior price levels*. I list those every morning. Remember: they include the pre-market high/low, the previous day high/low, and all the relevant daily price levels that I acquired from the daily chart.

For now you just need to understand that we're simply logging price levels that we find on the charts each morning. Essentially, we're logging simple numbers. For now you need to understand that these numbers are critical, and so is where and how you should log them.

I prefer to log them in my online trading room that I offer trainees and actively subscribed day traders, and also on my own whiteboards. I highly recommend that you do the same. Go get a whiteboard from Staples. It's about $20 for a 30″ × 40″ whiteboard. Or for now, just write on an 8″ × 11″ sheet of paper. Either way, hang it up on the wall. You save an entire LCD screen by doing so. No need to use up a screen when you have a whiteboard.

The point is to get all your numbers in order, to have those numbers correct, and to be ready to trade when that bell rings. You're going to learn that you can't possibly start trading unless you know your price numbers. That's why I'm making such a big deal of showing you how to gather and log the *prior* price levels.

Figure 2.11 is a screenshot of my whiteboard. I have many different scribblings on different days. This is just one example. I use one for each stock that I actively trade each day. This example happens to be LNKD. I logged both my pre-market and previous day high/low levels, and then I decided which daily levels should be on the chart for this given day.

Note that the pre-market levels are trading right around 231.00 (the pre-market high was 231.45 and pre-market low was 229.00). Also note the daily levels at the bottom of the whiteboard. The right-bottom column shows the daily low price levels, which will be used as my supports. The left-bottom column shows the daily high price

FIGURE 2.11 One of My Whiteboards

PRIOR PRICE LEVELS						
	Stock:	LNKD				
Pre market		Previous Day		Daily H/L		
Date:	1/23/15	Date:	1/22/15	HIGH		LOWS
HIGH	231.45	HIGH	226.00	239.17		214.52
				234.83		213.50
				232.28		209.60
LOW	229.00	LOW	217.14	230.15		204.22
	Stock:					
Pre market		Previous Day		Daily H/L		
Date:		Date:		Date:		Date:
HIGH		HIGH				
LOW		LOW				
	Stock:					
Pre market		Previous Day		Daily H/L		
Date:		Date:		Date:		Date:
HIGH		HIGH				
LOW		LOW				

FIGURE 2.12 Prior Price Levels

levels, which will be used as my resistance. I also use a *log sheet* for the prior price levels.

Notice the logged data in the first two columns in Figure 2.12. It corresponds with the data on the screenshot of the whiteboard on my wall. A whiteboard is important, but the log sheet is even more so. Keep one, and keep it filled in every day.

■ Log Your *Prior* Price Levels on a Whiteboard *Before* the Opening Bell

At this point it doesn't matter whether the price level is the premarket, previous day, or daily levels. What matters is having your prior price levels in *numerical order*. Have your support levels in one column and your resistance levels in another.

For the table shown in Figure 2.13 I simply transferred all the price levels from the LNKD stock example on the whiteboard and/or the log sheet, and then put them in descending order. The left column has the *high* (resistance) price levels, and the right column has all the *low* (support) price levels.

At this point I've shown you the basics of reading the daily chart and the one-minute chart, and how to gather all the *prior* price levels needed before the 9:30 A.M. bell at the New York Stock Exchange. In Chapter 3, I show you how to take these levels and trade them by using the 3-tier max system. For now you only need to absorb the process of gathering price levels.

Next I show you how to recognize the *newly forming price levels* that are created all day *after* the bell.

Learn how to recognize *newly forming* intra-day support/resistance.

HIGHS RESISTANCE LEVELS	LOWS SUPPORT LEVELS
239.17	229.00
234.83	217.14
232.28	214.52
231.45	213.50
230.15	209.60
226.00	204.22

FIGURE 2.13 High (Resistance) and Low (Support) Price Levels

Remember this rule: you need a *minimum of five consecutive one-minute candlesticks* to confirm a sustainable intra-day support/resistance level. This is because in the first five minutes after the bell rings, nothing will *form* to trade, because it takes at least that long for an intra-day level to take shape. After the first five minutes, you *may* have a stock that *may* have created the *first* intra-day support/resistance of the day.

Of course, this does *not* mean you won't trade the *prior* price levels within the first five minutes. Your initial trade of the day will most likely be traded off one of those. But if none of them breaks on your whiteboard and you don't have a trade during that window, then the thing to do is focus on the *newly* forming support/resistance levels, which must take at least the first five minutes after the bell.

Five *consecutive* candlesticks means that once you have an intra-day price run, at some point that price-run has to bottom or top, intra-day. This will happen in *one particular candlestick*. For instance, if you're forming an intra-day *support*, then the support price level will be the *lowest* price level of the *first* candlestick. If you're forming an intra-day *resistance*, then the resistance price level will be the *highest* price level of the *first* candlestick.

When I mention the *lowest/highest* price, I'm referring to the price level that's forming an *intra-day support/resistance*. You do not want the second, third, or fourth candlesticks *breaking* the *low* point of the *first* candlestick; this is what I mean by *consecutive* candlesticks. Likewise, if the price level is forming an intra-day resistance, you do not want the second, third, or fourth candlesticks breaking the *high* point of the *first* candlestick.

Also, each candlestick after the first can hit the *same* price level of the first, but it *can't break* its price level. If the second, third, or fourth *does* break the first candlestick's price level, then you have to start the process all over.

This is not as hard as it sounds. I provide you with illustrations that explain what all of this means. But of course, the best way to learn is hands-on, not just by reading this framework.

You might ask: "Which should be the first candlestick?" The first will be one of several that have previously dropped or climbed to an intra-day low or high. Whether the stock is forming an intra-day support or resistance, the first candlestick must be *higher* than the previous one when forming intra-day resistance and the first candlestick must be lower than the previous one when forming intra-day support. In other words, you need only *one* candlestick to hold to the left.

To reiterate:

- When forming intra-day *resistance*, the *first* candlestick must be *higher* than the previous one (use the *highest* price in each) as shown in Figure 2.14.

- When forming intra-day *support*, the *first* candlestick must be *lower* than the previous one (use the lowest price in each) as shown in Figure 2.15.

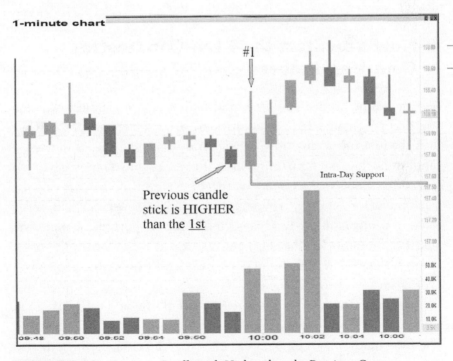

FIGURE 2.14 Previous Candlestick Higher than the Previous One

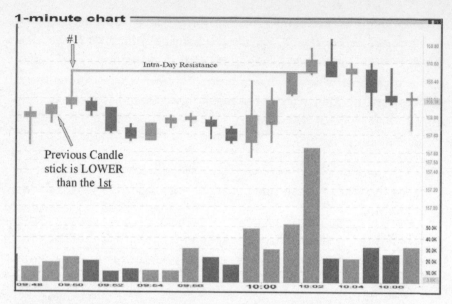

1-minute chart

#1

Intra-Day Resistance

Previous Candle
stick is LOWER
than the 1st

09:48   09:50   09:52   09:54   09:56   10:00   10:02   10:04   10:06

FIGURE 2.15   Previous Candlestick Lower than the Previous One

■ Now You Start the Five-Candlestick Counting Process

As I mentioned, once you've established your *first* candlestick, then you don't want the next candlestick to drop lower or climb higher than the first one at any time during its 60-second cycle. If the *second* candlestick does *not* drop/climb past the *first*, then you now have two *consecutive* candlesticks *holding* at the price level of the *first* (lowest price point for support, highest price point for resistance). In order to have a *sustained* newly formed intra-day support/resistance, the next *two* candlesticks (the third and the forth) *cannot* break the price point of the *first*. Again, if one does, you have to start the process all over again.

If all three candlesticks past the first candlestick don't break, then you need to focus on the *fourth* candlestick to the right of the first. The fifth candlestick cannot break the price level of the first. If you determine that the fifth candle has *confirmed* a newly formed intra-day support/resistance level, then you can prepare to place a trade off that price level. I elaborate this in Chapter 3.

■ How to Count Five Minimum Candlesticks (Chart Analysis)

In Figure 2.16 you have a newly formed intra-day *resistance* level at 157.76 at 9:36. This price level was never broken in the following four candlesticks. Therefore, once candle #5 never hits above 157.76 price level in candlestick #1, you had confirmation that the 157.76 price level (candlestick #1) was a new intra-day resistance level. Notice how it took eight minutes (or three candlesticks past the #5 candlestick) before it actually broke resistance.

For now, you should simply focus on recognizing the five minimum candlesticks that it requires to form a new intra-day support/resistance level. Also note that the 157.76 intra-day resistance level is the *current daily high*.

1-minute chart

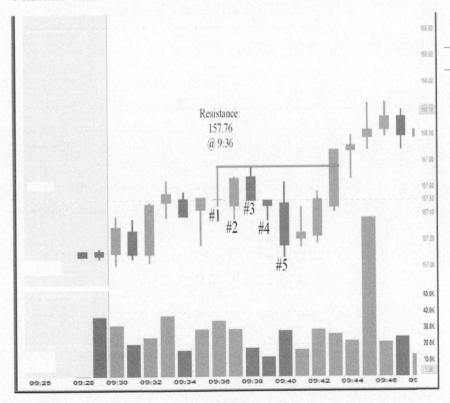

FIGURE 2.16   Five Minimum Candlesticks

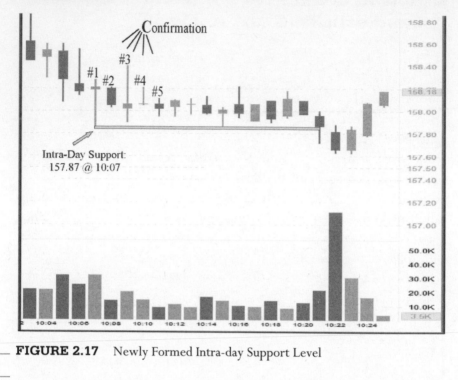

FIGURE 2.17 Newly Formed Intra-day Support Level

In Figure 2.17 you have an example of a newly formed intra-day *support* level at 157.87 at 10:07. The #1 candlestick bottomed at 157.87. The following four never broke this price level. Therefore we have our five minimum consecutive candlesticks. Note as well that the first candle to the left of #1 is higher. You can perceive that as a total of at least 6 candlesticks hooding at or above the support level.

■ Notes, Reminders, Cautions, and Hints of the Lessons to Come

- In Chapter 3, I show that you may have 20 intra-day levels at any given point throughout the day. But for now, *you will only be trading the intra-day highs and lows*. I've shown how you need the five-candlestick rule to form an intra-day high/low. In Chapter 3, I explain in greater detail why this is, but for now I emphasize the main reason: those price levels are relatively the *safest* to trade and the *easiest* to decipher.

- There is *no maximum or exact time frame* for a trade setup to take place, other than the entire day from 9:30 to 4:00. Typically, a new intra-day setup will develop within 5 to 15 minutes after each trade you place. Sometimes it can take an hour before a new one comes along. Even if you confirm an intra-day price level, it may take several minutes for an entry price level to hit. Some days are more volatile than others. The thing to remember is: *do not force trades*.

- If the price is trending in one direction, this means that each candlestick keeps dropping/climbing past the previous one. Thus you *do not* have the required five minimum *consecutive* candlesticks that form a new intra-day sustained support/resistance, even though you *may* be approaching one of the *prior* price levels: pre-market, previous day, and daily high/low.

## CHAPTER 3

Intra-Day Golden Rules: Entry/Exit Setups

Do *not* read this section without having read the previous sections first.

This chapter is hands-down the most fundamental step-by-step portion of my intra-day trading strategy. Before I begin, however, I want to make one crucial point crystal clear.

If you've fast-forwarded to this section without reading everything previous to it, then you will not grasp the material. You'll end up applying what I'm teaching with a one-dimensional viewpoint, and that's a recipe for disaster. If you are the reader I'm talking about, then I'll assume that you're seeking a quick-and-easy strategy to make huge profits right away. That is not going to happen. Anyone who promises that is scamming you, and that guy isn't me. So please go back and start from the beginning.

To the readers who've been with me since the first page of this book, my apologies for that tirade. But I have to lecture you a bit also. Even after thoroughly reading this section and committing every lesson to your memory, prior to going live with real money, you will need formal training. You can certainly test the system by paper trading, but it won't start to truly work for you until you've learned it hands-on.

I'll begin with the *Golden Rules*. Then I'll present guidelines and procedures that must be followed to the *T*.

> The following Golden Rules for intra-day trading apply to *each* and *every* trade.

The Golden Rules

Rule No. 1: Always know your second entry before you enter your first trade.

Rule No. 2: On all your initial trade setups, you must have at least one daily price level with $3 of your first entry—if not, then no initial trade.

Rule No. 3: You must have a maximum of three tiers for each trade setup (300 shares).

Rule No. 4: Your initial entry (first 100 shares) can be off any intra-day high/low or any prior level.

Rule No. 5: Never have two entries within 50 cents of each other.

Rule No. 6: When intra-day trading, your entry price will always be a static 25 or 50 cents past your chosen support/resistance level:

- 25 cents past intra-day high/low levels
- 50 cents past prior levels

All levels are 50 cents past up to 9:45 A.M. (the first 15 minutes of trading).

■ The Rules Explained

Rule No. 1: Always know your *second* entry *before* you enter your *first* trade.

This is all about preparation and self-discipline. Before you enter your *first* 100-share trade, it's imperative that you know your *second*. That sounds simple, right? But in order for this to work, you have to know your price levels, and that takes some planning and organizing.

The main purpose of this rule is to scrutinize your trading reflexes, to make you slow down and think extra hard about exactly what you're doing. It forces you to strategize with your price levels as the main plan.

If you just jump into a trade with no idea of what you'll do if it happens to run against you, then you're trading as blind as a bat. Remember: this system is countertrend. So chances are the price *will* run against you. When that occurs, simply find your lower/higher price levels.

Sometimes the price goes back into the green—sometimes within seconds. Great! You just made $15 in a heartbeat. But more likely your trade will run to the next tier. Your job is to be ready to reenter at your second or third tiers and then readjust your profit targets. In Chapter 4, I show you how to do that with fastkey order execution. For now, I just want you to absorb the fact that planning is everything.

A pro-trader's goal is to be very consistent and totally confident in his trades. If you plan for and enter any trade knowing that no matter what happens, you're prepared, then you are on the right path. Following this rule will provide you with psychological benefits. Once you master this system, after you enter a trade you will *never* be worried or scared. If I knew this back when I was a novice, I'd have far less gray hair now.

Amateurs mistakenly think that their first entry must bring a profit. If their initial trade doesn't go green right away, they get cold feet and they stop-loss. That's a great way to lose all your money. To be a pro-trader is to have a great plan, and no matter what happens, you're cool.

> **Rule No. 2:** On *all* of your *initial* trade setups, you must have *at least one daily price level* within *$3* of your *first* entry—if not, then *no* initial trade.

This rule is the absolute core of my new system, the *fusion* between intra-day and swing setups. The point of ensuring you have a daily price level within $3 of your first entry is to capture a *swing pivot* on your intra-day setups. That way, if your intra-day trade doesn't reverse for 15 cents (profit) by the close of the day, and you have to stop-loss on those shares, you *can hold your swing* 100-share position overnight and then recapture your loss the next morning by running the trade for a $2+ profit.

When I teach you my swing trading strategy, you will learn that certain daily price levels *are or become* swing levels. So intra-day trading by using daily levels is your first step toward mastering swing.

Of course, swing trades are much more involved than trading a daily level. I cover this in Part 3. For now I just want you to focus on the fact that you should *never* enter an intra-day trade unless you have a *defined* daily price level *within $3*. Figure 3.1 illustrates this.

The chart in Figure 3.1 shows how I waited until the price came up to 232.37, within $3 of the nearest *daily level* (at that time). Once the current price was within $3 of the next daily price level, I could start looking for resistance levels to trade.

Rule No. 3: You must have a *maximum* of *three tiers* for *each* trade setup (300 shares).

In my system, this rule is the main risk minimizer. This is the one rule that Wall Street doesn't follow. Of course not! I can

FIGURE 3.1 Daily Chart: LNKD

guarantee that Wall Street buy/sells much more than 300 shares per trade setup.

"But it can't be that way for me. I may be a professional but I'm not a whale trader—a guy with millions of dollars to trade." Very few traders are. Accordingly, most of us must limit our exposure to market risk. We cannot trade every single support/resistance level all throughout the day. For instance, our $100+ stocks can have as much as 20 intra-day support/resistance levels. Our job is to find the strongest three tiers (price levels) on each setup, which is not the same thing as trying to trade every strong level that forms.

This makes my system conservative. "*Conservative?*" you might ask with surprise. I'm aware that "conservative" applied to day trading sounds like an oxymoron. The word contradicts the dare to take risks, and people think day trading is dicey. But day trading is only high-risk if you trade at high-risk levels. The levels I trade at are strong and low-risk.

If you follow my coaching you'll place far fewer trades when waiting for those levels to hit, but once you add the swing trades I've added to my system, you won't be so caught up in placing 15-cent intra-day trades, because you'll also be capturing swing trades for $2 profits ($200 on each 100 shares). That's when you'll realize that "conservative" and "profit" can and do come together.

Another conservative measure is you *don't hold* an intra-day position overnight. That means if your trade doesn't go green, you have to stop-loss at the close. Not holding and limiting yourself to three tiers keeps your trading in check and forces you to trade the strongest levels. See how conservative can work here?

I prefer the word *safe*. My goal is to help you keep out of the poorhouse. I'm not saying I don't trade more than 300 shares intra-day, or more than 100 per tier; I'm talking about you, the novice. After you've mastered this system, on each of the three tiers you can trade more than 100 shares, but you do that on the swing system, not on the intra-day setups, and intra-day is where a beginner should start.

(Of course you'd rather *go big* (more than 300 shares) on swing trades for $2.00 profits, as opposed to 15 cents. But let's not get ahead of ourselves.)

Rule No. 4: Your *initial* entry (first 100 shares) can be off any *intra-day high/low* or any *prior* level.

Don't confuse this with Rule No. 3. That rule focuses primarily on the *daily price level* (always being within $3 of one), which is also a *prior* price level. With Rule No. 4 I'm pointing out that your initial entry can be off a newly formed high/low of day (intra-day level) or any of the other prior levels (pre-market high/low or previous day high/low).

In other words, your *first* entry can be off *any* of your whiteboard prior levels *during* the first five minutes of trading, or it can be *after* the first five minutes, when a new intraday high/low may have formed; that can also be your first entry. As long as you apply *all* of the Golden Rules, you can enter your first 100-share trade.

Rule No. 5: *Never* have two entries within *50 cents* of each other.

This rule is fairly straightforward. The main purpose here is to make sure your levels don't overlap, and to weed out the weaker of *two* possible support/resistance levels.

For instance, if you have a previous day high at 155.20 and a pre-market high of 155.50, you should not trade both because you may as well be entering the trade with 200 initial shares. When less than 50 cents apart, you're basically trading one price level. This is overexposure to risk. Also consider you only have three tiers (300 shares max), so it's important to choose your entry levels very conservatively. If you have two levels within 50 cents, always pick the stronger of the two.

In many cases you'll have more than four levels to choose from at any time throughout the trading session. I expand on this later. For now, here's a simple scenario to clarify this rule.

Suppose you have these four price levels:

155.20—Previous day high
155.50—Pre-market high
157.00—Newly formed intra-day high
157.25—Daily price level high

The current price is at 155.00, and is starting to shoot up. What price levels do you trade? Use the Golden Rules as your answer.

You need to have a daily price level within $3, and we have that here. But some of the levels are within 50 cents of each other. You always have to know your second entry before your first one, right? That's enough information to make your decision.

I would enter off the 155.50 level at my first entry because it's within $3 of the daily price level at 157.25. I would skip the first 155.20 because it's within 50 cents of 155.50, and I would skip the 157.00 intra-day high because that, too, is within 50 cents of 157.25.

Rule No. 6: When intra-day trading, your *entry price* will *always* be a static *25 or 50 cents past* your chosen support/resistance level.

25 cents past intra-day high/low levels
50 cents past prior levels

Note: All levels are *50 cents past* up to 9:45 A.M., the first 15 minutes of trading.

I list this rule last because you don't even consider applying it until you've utilized all the previous rules.

Your entries will *always* be either 25 or 50 cents *past* your price levels, with no exceptions. If you don't go 50 to 25 cents past, you risk making your entire 3-tier setup drastically off. Keep in mind that 50 cents times three 100-share entries is $150 (opportunity cost). Therefore, when utilized properly, this rule saves you $150.

You will soon learn the logic behind this. For now I can tell you that 95 percent of the time, your support/resistance price levels will get broken and run 25–50 cents past before they have a chance of reversing to profit target. This rule helps to absorb that incremental loss. This rule is the backbone of the *entry* strategy that I introduce in Part 3.

■ Mastering the Three-Tier Max Strategy with 100-Share Block Trades

Figure 3.2 represents the framework of my 3-tier setup. Note that the levels and entries follow the Golden Rules to the *T*.

You'll recall that this single directive to limit yourself to three tiers, or 300 shares, is 100 percent my own strategy. Wall Street

1-Minute Chart: 3-Tier Max Strategy

SHORT <u>3rd</u>
100 shares
209.42 @ 12:27

<u>DAILY</u> High (PRIOR Resistance) #3
208.92

<u>Previous Day</u> High (PRIOR Resistance) #2
208.40

SHORT <u>2nd</u>
100 shares
208.90 @ 12:16

<u>Intra-Day</u> High #1
207.85@ 9:50

Confirmation

SHORT <u>1st</u> 100 shares
208.10 @ 11:51

EXIT
(cover)
300 shares
208.66
@ 12:30

#1
#3
#2 #4
#5

AVERAGE PRICE
On 300 Share Setup
208.81

9:45 a 10:00 a 10:15 a 10:30 a 10:45 a 11:00 a 11:15 a 11:30 a 11:45 a 12:00 p 12:15 p 12:30 p 12:45 p

FIGURE 3.2 Three-Tier Max Strategy

pro-traders go much more than three tiers and they exceed 100 shares per entry. They can because they have millions, if not billions, of dollars. Do you? If not, then you should follow my directive, because it will keep you relatively safe.

Conservative price levels with small 100-share block trades means extremely overbought/oversold situations. Your focus on seeking 15-cent profits adds to the certainty of the overall trade making you bucks before the bell rings. If you're patient and you know your price levels, and you apply the Golden Rules with exacting precision, then your 3-tier setups will become $45 profits (15 cents times 300 shares) 90 percent of the time.

You might ask: "What about the other 10 percent of the time?" In Chapter 4 (the fusion on intra-day and swing), you'll learn how to take a 300-share intra-day loser and turn it into a winner. You'll find that you can do this by running it for a $2 profit off a major swing level. For now, however, I want you to focus on learning the intra-day basics.

In my hands-on training program, I have trainees *practice and not go live* with their intra-day setups. The reason why is at that stage, they take more losses than they should, mainly because they haven't yet learned how to turn things around with a swing trade. When they practice this intra-day strategy, and they're in the red after a 3-tier setup, I tell them to stop-loss by 4 P.M., when the closing bell rings.

"Why is this?" you might ask. "Why can't they *hold overnight?*" Because that was an intra-day level they were trading. It was only good for that day. Once you learn both strategies—both intra-day *and* swing—this will make a lot more sense. Such questions and head-scratching are proof of the wisdom of *not* thumbing ahead and reading out of order when you're tackling the material in this manual. Figure 3.2 illustrates how I use three price levels for my 3-tier max strategy.

■ Understanding the Wisdom of 15-Cent Static Profits

It just can't be said enough: you need to keep your profit targets consistent and conservative. In my system of intra-day trading, the 15-cent target is designed to achieve this. It happens to be the sweet-spot of numbers; because the market loves to trade off the general 25-cent barriers, the 15-cent max profit will never need to travel through more than one of them. In other words, if your exit price (15-cent profit target) does not break through two 25-cent barriers, then this increases the likelihood that you'll *quickly* gain a 15-cent profit. I explain this in depth later.

Also consider that when you trade through a pay-per-share broker, you can afford to make such a small profit off each of your 100-share trades. You should only be paying $1.00 max per execution in 100-share block trades. So after $1 to buy and $1 to sell, you net at least $13 on intra-day setups. Typically it will be a 2-tier setup or the max at 3-tier. So when you limit your profits to 15 cents, you'll earn $15—$45 on each trade.

Those stocks can fluctuate 15 cents in 10 seconds. That doesn't mean you earn $15 every 10 seconds. What it means is you've patiently waited for your target entry price to hit, and when it does your trade can go green very fast. (In order to make this work properly, you need fastkey order execution. I get to that in Chapter 4.)

The final point I want to make here is that you shouldn't be trying to earn more than 15 cents on any intra-day trade, because your goal is to hit the swing levels and run your trade for a hefty $2.00 profit ($200 on a 100-share trade). In essence, the smaller intra-day trades don't even have to be placed. You, as a beginner, need to master them first.

I view the intra-day setups as supplemental income. They help pass the time while I wait for the bigger and more profitable swing trades to trigger. Because I'm a seasoned trader, I rarely place intra-day trades for 15 cents anymore. These days, all my trades become swings because I plan it that way.

Eventually you'll be in my shoes. But you must learn to crawl before walking, and learning to swing is for sprinters. There is absolutely no fast-tracking this system, or for that matter *any* day trading system that deserves to be called valid or safe.

Figure 3.3 shows how it can take all morning to hit an intra-day setup, but within seconds it pulls back for the 15-cent profit. So your trade can profit in no time, but before it triggers you're required

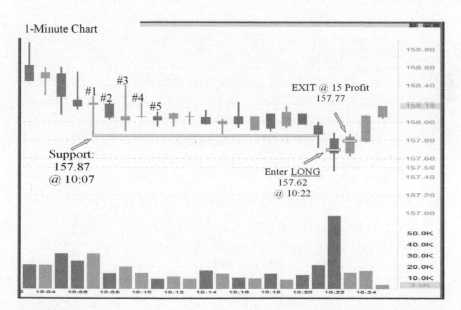

FIGURE 3.3 One-Minute Chart

to do considerable waiting and planning. This chart also shows how it took over 15 minutes for the intra-day level to form, and then it finally broke. After I entered the trade, it profited 15 cents in the next candlestick, less than one minute later. Note that the price kept going higher, after I exited.

You might ask: "Why didn't you hold on longer for more profit?" I love it when I'm asked that 20/20-hindsight question. First, how the heck can you know it was going to continue more than the 15 cents? If you could predict that with certainty on every trade setup, you'd be a billionaire! Looking at a chart afterwards is easy, but trading in real time is a whole other beast.

I had no clue it was going to continue to rise, but I did know that my 15-cent target was very likely to hit. The lesson here is don't get greedy! Stick with 15-cent profits on intra-day setups. If not, you will chance toward that slippery slope of inconsistent trading. For instance, if you start to allow your profits to run to 20 cents, 30 cents, 50 cents, I can guarantee that you're going to lose big and never become a pro-trader. If you try to get even 20 cents on each intra-day setup, several of your trades will hit 18 cents in the green and then tumble all the way back down and you'll hold a losing trade all day. And if you're truly a haphazard trader, you'll *hold* that losing position overnight. Does the gambling mentality come to mind here?

In that scenario, all you had to do was take your 15 cents and be happy. Your trade hit 18 cents in the green, but you just had to have 20. Consider how silly that is. Why would you risk an additional 5 or even 10 more cents in profit (or try to get 20–25 cents each trade) when you're waiting on a swing setup that will get you a full $2.00 profit? When you learn to do swing trades, this will instantly make sense.

■ Observing the Framework of Entry and Exit Strategy with Step-by-Step Procedures and Guidelines

Before I jump into the steps, here are some basic pointers. I've said it before and I'll say it again: you're looking at the map here, not the road; I *cannot* say "this is only the framework" enough.

Each stock you acquire and begin to trade with my system will have to be tweaked a bit. As I mentioned previously, some stocks move faster than others; some stocks have fewer tiers to trade; some stocks react differently at swing levels, and so on. The point is my guidelines are general. These lessons don't apply across the board. This is a major reason why you need to be formally trained. Even after I train you, it will take you some time to get married to your stocks. It's all about patience and due diligence. I'm sorry, but I can't offer a simple, straightforward golden-goose strategy. There is no such thing.

Previously I briefly went over the *general market price barriers*: .25–.50–.75–.00. In this section I map the generalities on when to enter/exit an intra-day trade. I've shown you how to gather your *whiteboard* (prior) price levels, and I've shown you how to confirm a *newly formed intra-day high/low* (the 5-candlestick rule for resistance/support). Now you just need to know what price to enter at once your prior or new levels break.

Remember the number-one principle of reverse-countertrend trading: we only enter *after* our predefined price levels break. And remember this Golden Rule: you enter your trade at exactly *25 cents* or *50 cents* past your *entry* price level.

You won't be required to trade using the general market price barrier technique, but it does help to reinforce why I go 25 and 50 cents *past* S/R levels:

- Every *25 cent level* is a standard/general market price barrier, whether you're entering or exiting a trade.

- There's general market resistance, regardless of intra-day support/resistance levels, when the stock breaks through these price levels:

$125.00–$125.25–$125.50–$125.75

My system of entry/exit points is based on the probability that once an intra-day support/resistance level breaks, and the price continues to travel past that intra-day level, the *next* general price barrier is the *very next 25-cent level*. So if you enter a countertrend trade *after* this overbought/oversold price level, then you're likely to see the price *reverse* 15 cents into the green.

Also consider that when the price runs on our $100–$250 high-priced stocks, they've reached extremely overbought/oversold intra-day levels. This happens in a relatively short amount of time. Since their previous intra-day high/low price levels, they most likely have traveled $1 to $3. Therefore, your 15-cent profit target is very conservative.

What does this mean? The price run is 10 times more likely to reverse for a quick 15 cents than to travel another $3 parabolic price hike. Therefore, it's important for you to understand why you should wait for the price to run the full 25 to 50 cents. I've made some basic rules for both entry and exit to help it all click.

Rule of Entry:
> When the intra-day support/resistance price level has been *broken* (the one you chose by using the Golden Rules), you want to *enter* the trade on the *initial* time it breaks past that level by exactly 25 or 50 cents.

Rule of Exit:
> Once you've *entered* a trade, you exit on the *initial* time it hits your 15-cent profit target.

Think about it: if you need to break a 25-cent general market barrier on your entry, then all you need to do is go 25 cents past the support/resistance price level. If you're exiting, then my static 15-cent profit target satisfies the rule of exit. But again, you won't enter 25 or 50 cents past with all stocks or all situations, especially when you learn the swing strategy. In swing you will go as much as $1–$2 past certain price levels. When I say the word *initial*, I cannot stress it enough.

When the price approaches *your target entry/exit price,* you should be waiting for it to hit the *first* time in real-time. When the price *initially* hits, you should either be entering or exiting the trade. As I've mentioned before, *fastkey order execution* is the tool you need here, and teaching you that will be part of my instruction.

■ Entry Strategy

Figures 3.4 and 3.5 are for both *support and resistance* levels. The charts show the general idea of countertrend reverse trading and how you're

Intra-Day Entry Levels: <u>SUPPORT</u>

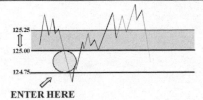

If actual support
level is at **125.00** then
LONG entry is **124.75**

FIGURE 3.4   Intra-Day Entry Levels: Support

Intra-Day Entry Levels: <u>RESISTANCE</u>

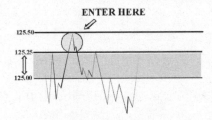

If actual resistance
level is at **125.25** then
SHORT entry is **125.50**

FIGURE 3.5   Intra-Day Entry Levels: Resistance

breaking through a general market barrier on every trade. They also illustrate the fact that you enter on the *initial* breakout.

■ Exit Strategy

When you enter a trade you must *always* hold the position for *at least a 15-cent profit* ($15 profit on each 100-share block) before you *exit*.

On the chart setup in Figure 3.6 I illustrate how to apply the exit strategy.

I entered a short position at 158.72. This was exactly 25 cents above the newly formed intra-day level of 158.47. Within seconds after I entered the trade, the price pulled back for 15 cents for my profit target. I exited at 158.67.

At first glance this looks like a simple cookie-cutter setup. You will see this similar pattern all over your intra-day one-minute charts. Had

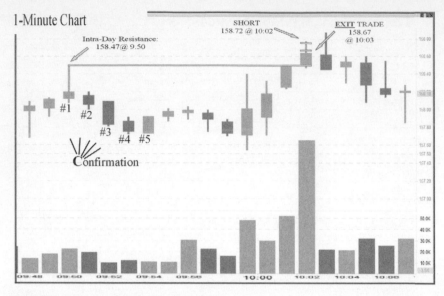

FIGURE 3.6 One-Minute Chart

I not known how to use fastkey, however, this trade would have been missed, and could have kept going higher.

Implement the Golden Rules before *every* trade, exit on the *initial* price hit of your 15-cent profit target, learn fastkey order execution, and you've mastered the beginning of my system.

■ The Wisdom of Using Strategy Stop-Loss

No novice day trader likes to place a stop-loss. But as I've told you before, all pro-traders understand that it's a normal part of the day trading process. During my discussion of updates and changes, I initially mentioned that my current system redefines stop-loss. It changes how or when you should execute one, and I call it *strategy stop-loss*.

To those readers who have been under my mentorship, I want to remind you again that I *no longer use* nominal value stop-loss exits. Now that I use swing trades as major pivot points, it makes absolutely no sense to stop-loss when I'm $XXX in the red. Instead, when accumulating a position, I capture even stronger levels. This I clarify later. For now I'll show some examples of strategy stop-loss in some easily defined situations.

When it comes to applying a stop-loss, intra-day trades are different from swing trades. As you know, you *cannot hold* an intra-day trade overnight, so you have to close the intra-day positions before the bell rings at 4:00 P.M. Therefore, you must get accustomed to taking a short-term loss on some trades. This does *not* mean your net trade is a complete loss. I explain this in Part 5 when I discuss pivot trading versus stop-loss.

The most common situation where I *strategy-stop-loss* is—you guessed it—at the closing bell. As I've mentioned before, this doesn't apply in swing trading. Swing positions you can hold overnight.

Remember that when you use my system, you *do not* exit at a loss simply because the price runs against you. This may be hard to swallow, because in most cases the price *will* run against you. This is totally normal with my system and you need to get used to it.

"Why?" you may ask, totally puzzled. This point may be difficult to grasp, because this system—no matter whether intra-day or swing—will show you that if you're in the red, then you're about to hit even stronger entry levels, those levels you need to enter at; *so why would you be exiting at a loss when you should be adding to your current trade at stronger price levels?* The answer to this question will take time and experience to know. Even after learning the framework here, this is by far one of the most critical reasons why you can't learn this system entirely on paper.

Chances are you've been taught to stop-loss when down a certain amount or percentage. That's how most amateurs trade. *In my training program, you learn the exact opposite.* As I initially mentioned in this book, you need to be reprogrammed, and I can't do that without coaching you, and I can't coach you on paper.

The hardest part of this system is not getting scared when in the red. To be a real day trader, you need thick skin. Most traders who attempt this without formal training make the same mistake: they cut their profits early, break even, or simply stop-loss when deep in the red. On the contrary, when you're using my system, you'll find that if you'd held a bit longer and added to your position at key levels, then that would have been a profit.

I'm sure you've had this happen: you exit a trade at a loss, and 10 minutes later or a day later the stock price reverses back to the green, but you left it already, so no dice. I can promise your fear will make this happen to you if you don't master this system. Even advanced traders in my one-year program still struggle with this psychological barrier.

Remember: this is countertrend trading. I don't expect it to make much sense right now, but I promise that later you'll understand why I don't use nominal values or percentages to determine a stop-loss exit. Think about it. If I were to stop-loss every time I got $3 in the red ($300 loss on 100 shares), then about 90 percent of all my past profitable trades would be losses instead, to date.

In the swing strategy section you'll learn that you should start intra-day trading positions once your intra-day setups are within $3 of your swing entry. Again, this does not mean you simply enter a trade once you're within $3 of a swing level. It certainly isn't that easy.

For now I want to get you used to intra-day trading while in the red as much as $3. That translates to $300 in the red when holding a 100-share position. This is perfectly normal when you use my full system, which means you're setting up your intra-day trades so that they hit swing levels. In Chapter 4, I show you this *fusion*.

For now you just need to internalize these hard-to-digest truths: that you *never hold your intra-day positions overnight*, and you may have to stop-loss on them at the close.

Below is the list of directives you read in Part 1. As a trainer I've learned that *not* following these tips is the main reason why many fail at day trading, so I've decided repetition is an aid.

- Always have a predetermined exit strategy. *Never* hold an intra-day position past 4:00 P.M. at market close. *Never* hold overnight.

- If you accumulate more of a swing position intra-day and are using margin/leverage, then you must stop-loss the amount of shares on margin. (Later I introduce what I call *pivot trading*. This strategy allows you the opportunity to recapture the amount lost today on the very next market opening.)

- *Never* hold any position into an earnings release (typically in aftermarket trading). Exit your entire position by 4:00 P.M. on the day of earnings release. This is especially true for swing positions that you *can* hold overnight—just never into earnings release. It's way too risky to hold into a release, because once Wall Street starts trading, the stocks we trade can easily fluctuate $30+ in either direction. That's a $3,000 loss, even with only 100 shares, if you get the call wrong.

■ Never allow standard stock-related news to dictate your entry/exit process, except when your stock is literally hitting the "breaking news" wire on MSNBC. Combined with other factors, such as the volume on the stock and how many shares and which tiers you're in, only then should you think about just exiting when in the red. If you're in the green, that's great, but if not, that's a classic time to stop-loss.

The above almost never happens with my stocks. Most news is already factored into the price, so breaking news has to be truly in the moment and devastating, or otherwise hugely impacting, for me to stray from my plan.

An example of strategy stop-loss would be a CEO giving notice of stepping down, or when mergers are announced. Again, these things almost never happen with our $100+ stocks, so stop-loss caused by the news is very uncommon with my system.

The most prevalent reason for strategy stop-loss is actually the easiest to follow. I've mentioned it before, and I'll box it up for emphasis this time.

> If you know you made a mistake by entering at the wrong price level, then stop-loss. It's that simple.

## CHAPTER 4

The Mechanics of FASTKEY Order Execution

Your intra-day trades are for only 15 cents. In some cases, such trades form in milliseconds. Because of this, fastkey is essential.

You'll find that when you aren't using fastkey, your back-testing will show you that several of your setups are in the green, but you didn't profit. The reason is it happened so fast that you didn't place an exit order when you should have. This is what makes fastkey so crucial.

I know I sound like a broken record when I say that this topic is by far the hardest to teach on paper, and certainly impossible to master without weeks of hands-on practice. This is the single largest reason why new day traders lose on their intra-day trades. Not utilizing proper fastkey procedure will result in poor intra-day trading.

■ Using Your Keyboard Keys for Rapid Order Execution

Figure 4.1 is an illustration of a normal PC or laptop keyboard, and the option it has for placing trades. It makes order execution 10 times faster.

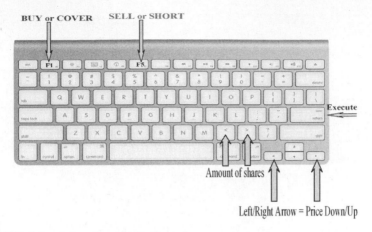

FIGURE 4.1   PC or Laptop Keyboard

Most broker platforms have this function, but very few are true direct access.

■ Placing Orders Directly from a Level 2 Quote Chart (Direct Access)

You can order directly from the *Level 2* streaming quote chart. Having said that, I also want to make it clear that I can certainly tell you about fastkey, but I can't show you how to set it up, not here, not on paper, in a manual. You won't be able to practice it right until you're in my training program and you're working with my custom demo layout.

Trying to learn fastkey on paper without using the demo platform is like reading a flight manual and then trying to fly a real plane, without training first in a flight simulator. So, for now, let's just focus on the concept.

The following three charts in Figures 4.2 to 4.4 show snapshots of what your Level 2 quote charts should look like. They include *buy/cover*, *sell/short*, and *limit* orders.

Note how the order box (the small applet window to the upper left) is capable of directly executing trades. The applet window is the small box that pops up when you press either F1 or F5. This box is green when you buy long or cover short and red when you sell or you short.

FASTKEY Order Execution

Key Functions

F1 = BUY / COVER (Green applet window pops-up)
F5 = SELL / SHORT (RED applet window pops-up)
Esc = clear all open orders
Enter = execute order now
Left/Right arrow key = changes price in applet window

To BUY / COVER: PRESS F1 key

Your price in the applet window defaults to show the current BID.

To get immediately filled:
Make the price in applet window match the current Ask price (160.21), then press ENTER to get order filled.

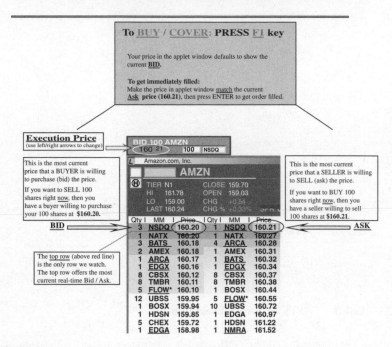

Execution Price (use left/right arrows to change)

This is the most current price that a BUYER is willing to purchase (bid) the price.

If you want to SELL 100 shares right now, then you have a buyer willing to purchase your 100 shares at **$160.20**.

This is the most current price that a SELLER is willing to SELL (ask) the price.

If you want to BUY 100 shares right now, then you have a seller willing to sell 100 shares at **$160.21**.

The top row (above red line) is the only row we watch. The top row offers the most current real-time Bid / Ask.

FIGURE 4.2 FASTKEY Order Execution #1

The applet window has a *market maker box*. In the diagram examples, the box has NSDQ as the market channel the current trade will be routed through. Don't worry about this box. You can keep it as NSDQ when demo trading and/or trading live. Either way, your orders will get filled when your price hits, in most cases.

There certainly are several variables that can make your trades very difficult to fill, even with the aid of fastkey. For instance, if you throw a 5,000-share order at the market, it's not going to fill right away, and it will most likely be a partial fill. This is one more reason why

FASTKEY Order Execution

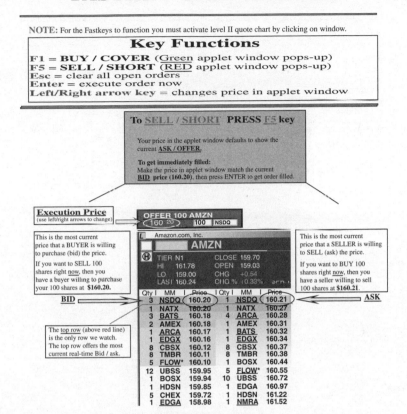

Key Functions

F1 = BUY / COVER (<u>Green</u> applet window pops-up)
F5 = SELL / SHORT (<u>RED</u> applet window pops-up)
Esc = clear all open orders
Enter = execute order now
Left/Right arrow key = changes price in applet window

To SELL / SHORT PRESS F5 key

Your price in the applet window defaults to show the current **ASK / OFFER**.

To get immediately filled:
Make the price in applet window match the current **BID price (160.20)**, then press ENTER to get order filled.

Execution Price
(use left/right arrows to change)

OFFER 100 AMZN
160 20 | 100 | NSDQ

This is the most current price that a BUYER is willing to purchase (bid) the price.

If you want to SELL 100 shares right <u>now</u>, then you have a buyer willing to purchase your 100 shares at **$160.20**.

BID

The top row (above red line) is the only row we watch. The top row offers the most current real-time Bid / ask.

This is the most current price that a SELLER is willing to SELL (ask) the price.

If you want to BUY 100 shares right <u>now</u>, then you have a seller willing to sell 100 shares at **$160.21**.

ASK

Amazon.com, Inc.
AMZN

TIER N1		CLOSE 159.70
HI 161.78		OPEN 159.03
LO 159.00		CHG +0.54
LAST 160.24		CHG % 0.33%

Qty	MM	Price	Qty	MM	Price
3	NSDQ	160.20	1	NSDQ	160.21
1	NATX	160.20	1	NATX	160.27
3	BATS	160.18	4	ARCA	160.28
2	AMEX	160.18	1	AMEX	160.31
1	ARCA	160.17	1	BATS	160.32
1	EDGX	160.16	1	EDGX	160.34
8	CBSX	160.12	8	CBSX	160.37
8	TMBR	160.11	8	TMBR	160.38
5	FLOW*	160.10	1	BOSX	160.44
12	UBSS	159.95	5	FLOW*	160.55
1	BOSX	159.94	10	UBSS	160.72
1	HDSN	159.85	1	EDGA	160.97
5	CHEX	159.72	1	HDSN	161.22
1	EDGA	158.98	1	NMRA	161.52

FIGURE 4.3 FASTKEY Order Execution #2

we don't trade with much more than 100 shares per entry. Even at my level of experience, I very rarely enter with more than 500 shares on any given price level.

Even if you have $5 million in buying power, and you want to and *can* place a 5,000-share order, it's not going to work.

"Why not?" you might ask. Because your own order will push the price higher/lower, making partial fills, and that is no good. If your orders are constantly partially filled, your consistency goes right out the window.

Notice the price level of AMZN. At the $160 level, the charts must be old, but that's okay, the concept never changes.

NOTE: For the Fastkeys to function you must activate level II quote chart by clicking on window.

Key Functions

F1 = BUY / COVER (Green applet window pops-up)
F5 = SELL / SHORT (RED applet window pops-up)
Esc = clear all open orders
Enter = execute order now
Left/Right arrow key = changes price in applet window

LIMIT ORDERS: PRESS F1 or F5

Place your price in applet window UNDERSIDE of the current BID or ASK price.

If you are going LONG, then make price LOWER then BID price.

If you are going SHORT, then make price HIGHER then ASK price.

PRESS ENTER, and your order will become a LIMIT order in the ORDERS window.

LIMIT Price
(press enter and 160.08 becomes limit order)

This is the most current price that a BUYER is willing to purchase (bid) the price.

If you want to SELL 100 shares right now, then you have a buyer willing to purchase your 100 shares at **$160.20**.

This is the most current price that a SELLER is willing to SELL (ask) the price.

If you want to BUY 100 shares right now, then you have a seller willing to sell 100 shares at **$160.21**.

The top row (above red line) is the only row we watch. The top row offers the most current real-time Bid / Ask.

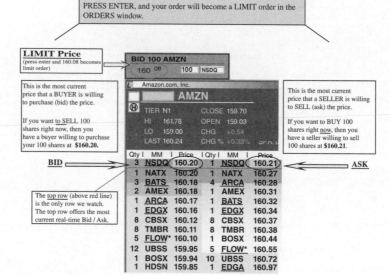

BID 100 AMZN
160 08   100   NSDQ

Amazon.com, Inc.
AMZN
TIER N1   CLOSE 159.70
HI   161.78   OPEN 159.03
LO   159.00   CHG   +0.54
LAST 160.24   CHG % +0.33%

Qty	MM	Price	Qty	MM	Price
3	NSDQ	160.20	1	NSDQ	160.21
1	NATX	160.20	1	NATX	160.27
3	BATS	160.18	4	ARCA	160.28
2	AMEX	160.18	1	AMEX	160.31
1	ARCA	160.17	1	BATS	160.32
1	EDGX	160.16	1	EDGX	160.34
8	CBSX	160.12	8	CBSX	160.37
8	TMBR	160.11	8	TMBR	160.38
5	FLOW*	160.10	1	BOSX	160.44
12	UBSS	159.95	5	FLOW*	160.55
1	BOSX	159.94	10	UBSS	160.72
1	HDSN	159.85	1	EDGA	160.97

BID ← → ASK

FIGURE 4.4   FASTKEY Order Execution #3

■ Executing Real-Time Trades (Manual *Limit* Orders)

My system of order entry is based on real-time limit orders, or manual limit orders, "manual" meaning you do it yourself; you don't have a system or program placing any trades for you. Whether you're buying or selling at a profit or a loss, your fastkey orders will *all* be in real time, and *always* placed manually.

THE MECHANICS OF FASTKEY ORDER EXECUTION

After reading Chapter 3 you should know how to scrutinize one-minute candlestick intra-day charts and also your prior price levels, and you should know how to find the exact entry/exit price by adding or subtracting by 25 or 50 cents. "*Wow!* That sounds so easy," you may be thinking. But I can assure you it's not. And that truth becomes even truer when you do this with more than one stock.

Easy? Yeah, right; assuming that you've been onboard this whole time and know your entry/exit prices perfectly, then all you need to do at this point is tap on the left/right arrow key right before you press Enter, execute your limit order in real time—and *voila!* You're done! Now you're gonna make some money.

I'm kidding. We have a long way to go.

You may wonder why we call it a "limit" order. If it's going to fill within seconds of placement, isn't that a market order?

That is a good question. Most traders are accustomed to placing limit orders rather than market orders. Typically, when you're swing trading and you place a standard limit order, the order price is more than 25 cents off the current market price, usually a dollar or more, and it could take hours or even days before it's hitting/filling. So most traders associate "limit order" with waiting for extended periods before entering/exiting a trade. Something that fills within seconds can't be a limit order, right?

Wrong. The previous fastkey diagram on limit orders represents the following scenario: the applet window (F1 to *buy*) reads *$160.08*. Notice that it's 12 cents *below the current bid* of $160.20. When I hit Enter the price will execute a buy order, making it a *temporary* limit order. The order for $160.08 will not fill until the *current ask price* of $160.21 comes down to $160.08.

"How long does this take?" you might ask. That's another good question. It depends. The closer you try to get your fill price to the current bid/ask, the quicker it will fill. In this case, the execution price to buy long was $160.08. That means the current trade had a support price level of 160.33 (25 cents above 160.08). I placed the order for 160.08 as soon as it broke the 160.33 level.

This is a great strategy because it gives you some time to get your order out there. Typically the price will not drop 25 cents in less than five seconds—and five seconds is an eternity when you need to get an order out fast. So when you're intra-day trading, you *never* keep an order open for more than one minute. With my system you're going to rapidly find that once your levels break and you choose a price level to enter/exit, *your price will be a limit order for less than one minute.*

Tapping your left/right arrow key is the mechanics of fastkey. For instance: if you were buying *long*, then you'd want to press Enter after *pressing the left arrow key enough times* to get the execution price in the applet window to be *lower* than the current *bid* price.

That sums up the fastkey portion of coaching. Again, all I can offer here on paper is the non-mechanical aspects. You truly will not understand how fastkey order execution works until you are applying it in real-time.

■ Scrutinizing Both Real-Time and End-of-Day Trades with Back-Testing

Back-testing is the *glue* of my system. This process helps to reinforce my entire trading methodology. If you're not back-testing properly, then you are not progressing.

When you're back-testing either demo or live real-time trades, you're reverse-engineering each previous roundtrip trade and reviewing and reconfirming each previous and newly forming intra-day support/resistance in real time.

You've most likely practiced back-testing of some form in the past. The difference is that now you have a clear system to refer to. Once you completely understand my trading methodology, you're ready to learn to do back-testing properly.

First, you need to have a platform that can *scroll back in time on the one-minute candlestick chart.* You need to be able to view the current day and previous day's candlesticks on a one-minute chart. Most platforms lack those functions. They can't scroll back or pan back on the one-minute candlestick chart and they don't allow you to see each one clearly. The platforms that do have those functions usually cost $100–$300 per month, such as *TradeStation*, *ThinkorSwim*, and *Esignal*.

Don't worry; I have a *free* option for you. Go to www.Free StockCharts.com.

I urge you to register with this market data provider. Other than a vertical advertising banner on the right side of the chart, there are absolutely no strings. I jokingly tell my trainees to just grab some duct tape and cover it up. The software downloads in seconds and you will be impressed. Please be warned, however: the *FreeStockCharts* platform is for back-testing *only*. *Do not* attempt to use their charts for *real-time* trading and charting.

"Why not?" you might ask. You obviously need real-time charting for my system to work properly when you trade. When back-testing, however, at end-of-day trading, the data doesn't need to be in real-time; you just need it to have correct data. For instance, once a one-minute candlestick closes on *FreeStockCharts*, the high/low prices are logged as actual price levels (the correct closing high/low prices in each candlestick). But when you view the most current candlestick in real time, you *don't* receive direct access information up to the millisecond. For real-time data, you use your broker's charts.

Figure 4.5 is a screenshot of the *FreeStockCharts* platform. You will have to perform some basic setting changes to get your data to look like the chart.

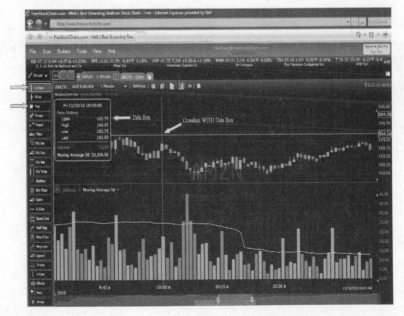

FIGURE 4.5 FreeStockCharts Platform

Take note that the arrows will be yellow. These are the only functions you will ever need to use on this platform. You will use the "cross" and "pan" tabs to the left. You will use your left mouse/click button to drag/pan the screen to the left or right.

Make sure your candlesticks are set to one minute and add another tab for your *daily* candlestick chart. The data box will give you the *exact* high/low price for each candlestick.

Here are two applications for back-testing.

1. To scrutinize your real-time (current) intra-day trading activity.

    My system is based on knowing all the *prior* support/resistance (S/R) price levels, and particularly your *newly* forming intra-day S/R price levels. Therefore, real-time back-testing is a pivotal process to determine what price levels are correct to trade off of, either in the moment or in real time.

    Basically, real-time back-testing is looking at your charts and scrutinizing the current day's trading. It helps you to recognize newly forming support/resistance levels throughout the current trading session.

    When intra-day trading in real time on your broker's platform, you can back-test on their one-minute chart. This is because the candlesticks can fit on one screen, for one full day of trading activity. Accordingly, I always recommend to my trainees to buy at least one 27-inch or greater monitor. The one-minute candlesticks get smaller and smaller throughout the day, so having a larger and wider screen allows you to back-test by viewing with the naked eye—no need to pan or scroll back.

    Once you get more advanced, you will find this is critical. You won't have time to be back-and-forth-back-and-forth when you're caught up in active trading. And I can almost guarantee that you'll miss previous intra-day S/R levels if you're not viewing the entire day on one screenshot.

    Budget for a couple of 27-inch or greater LCD screens *before* you go live. I promise this will save you a lot of grief. If you currently have a split-screen setup, this will work as well, but you'll have to stretch the one-minute chart across two screens. This will create a thick border down the middle of your chart.

That border can play tricks with your eyes. It's fine to keep your nice two-, four-, or six-way split setup with screens that are 17 inches, but you should add at least two 27-inch or greater screens and use them exclusively for the one-minute candlestick chart, because you can stretch the whole chart across this screen during pre-market trading and all day. You should always see the one-minute candlesticks *clearly*.

2. To scrutinize your *end-of-day* intra-day trading activity and to commit to it as if it were homework.

Here are the primary questions you should ask yourself:

Did I have all my prior levels on the whiteboard?
Was my original entry price the correct intra-day S/R level?
Was I in rhythm with the volume bars at the time of the trade?
Did I simply falter at the fastkey?
Did I properly use the Golden Rules?
Did I miss a tier in my three-tier setup?
Did I place a static entry/exit price and walk away from trade?
Did I hesitate on initial breakout and then chase trade?
Was I impatient and frustrated at time of entry?
Was I simultaneously in more than one trade?
Can I view the entire trading session (one-minute candlesticks) on one screen?
What obvious mistake(s) can I remember having made?

It's best to back-test your trades when they're still very fresh in your mind. When using *FreeStockCharts*, you can easily set the chart to one minute and then pan or scroll back to the time of your first trade entry on the day before and/or earlier that same day. You can either back-test at the end of the day, or you can back-test the next morning, meaning, if you placed intra-day trades on Thursday, and on Friday morning you're back-testing, you scroll back on the one-minute chart to Thursday.

When you use the *Lightspeed* demo in my training program, you'll be able to print out your orders. Your order window will log all the critical data you need for you to back-test properly. For instance, it has columns. The data you'll need for back-testing is very basic, such as stock symbol, order execution time, number of shares, price in/out, and position (long/short). Simply find your entry/exit points on the one-minute chart, and begin back-testing your trades according to my trading system.

The sole purpose of back-testing your previous (end-of-day) trades is to learn from your mistakes and reinforce your improvements. This goes without saying, but I say it anyway, because repetition always works, and reprogramming you is my job.

You've learned the entire framework of my intra-day trading system. You've learned it without knowing swing trading setups. I've taught you this way because it's hard enough to learn my intra-day system by itself. I've separated the two so you'll master the two before I show you the fusion of both.

I highly recommend that you go back to the beginning of this chapter and *reread it* before moving on to Part 3, in which I show you the swing trading framework. That way you'll know the rules for each type of trade so well that you won't confuse them and/or overlap them.

## PART III

DAY TRADER JOSH'S SWING TRADING METHODOLOGY

Warning: After reading the Table of Contents, chances are this is the section that impatient traders will thumb to. If that's you, please go back to the beginning of this manual and start your reading from there. Any attempt to fast-forward to here and start at this section on swing trading will result in confusion and/or gross misconstruing and misuse of my system. The end result will be financial loss.

## CHAPTER 5

Introduction to Swing Trading: Basic Rules and Procedures

> Your *daily chart* price levels help to determine your swing levels.

At this point, it's crucial for you to already know the intra-day portion of this system. If not, you won't grasp and adequately apply the instructions on swing trading essentials that follow.

If you've studied the previous section, then you've learned how to use the *daily* price levels when finding the intra-day setups, and you've also learned how to apply the intra-day Golden Rules. Without them, you won't enter swing levels properly. Why? The intra-day levels help to determine your adjusted swing levels. Without them, your swing entries will be as much as $1 or more off.

This is more fully explained in Part 4, where I introduce you to *fusion*. In this part, which I've broken into two separate chapters to help you conceptualize, you'll learn the more profitable, yet more risky, swing trading strategy.

"Why is it more risky than intra-day trading?" you might want to know. It is because you're *holding* overnight and potentially with more than 300 shares. So swing trading is much more advanced than intra-day. Whether I formally coach you or you risk it alone, either way, it takes weeks to master.

In this part of the text I show only swing trading setups. Again, you'll learn how to merge intra-day trades with swing trades in Part 4 on *fusion*. For now my main goal is to show you how to recognize which levels are swing levels and which swing tiers you should enter at.

Let's get started on technical instructions. Just as in Part 2, where you learned to gather intra-day *daily price levels*, you'll need to set your chart to view *daily* candlesticks. You'll see that some of the price levels you've acquired for intra-day setups also happen to be swing levels. In this chapter I specifically show you how a daily price level can become a swing level.

But first let's recap the rules regarding how to pick daily price levels. It's important to be redundant here so I can reinforce just how critical your daily chart price levels are.

You have two basic price levels: your daily lows (supports) and your daily highs (resistance). To find them on the *daily chart*, you start with these procedures:

- To find the *daily lows*, look at the most current day on the candlestick chart and scan to the left until you find the first candle that has *at least four higher* candlesticks to its *left and right*, meaning the price level has held for at least nine trading sessions.

  This typically resembles a "V" shape.

- To find the *daily highs*, look at the most current day on the candlestick chart and scan to the left until you find the first candle that has *at least four lower* candlesticks to its *left and right*, meaning the price level has held for at least nine trading sessions.

  This typically resembles a "pyramid" shape.

Recall that each price level has at least *four candlesticks* on each side of the daily price level. This means the price held for *at least nine days straight* without breaking that level.

Once you start gathering the proper price levels, you'll find that there are several that match this criterion. You'll find that using this simple system on the daily chart produces several results for both supports and resistance.

Here is a recap of the rules that will help you eliminate several *weaker* daily levels:

■ Each daily level should be *$1.00 or more* than the other.

■ If you have two or more daily price levels within $1.00 of each other, then you choose the lowest/highest.

And you disregard levels that are over a year old. *Unless*:

■ The price level *was or is an all-time high/low*.

■ It has *over 30 days* to its left and right.

■ It's *over two years old*. Then it must be *more than $5.00* off other daily levels.

Following is an introduction to the breakdown on swing rules.

■ Introducing the Ten-Day Hold Rule

Before you can consider a daily price level a swing level, and therefore your current swing level to trade, each *daily level* needs to hold for at least 10 consecutive days. That's *10 consecutive trading sessions*.

For example:

■ If a new daily level forms that day, you need to wait five more days before it can be traded, *10 days total* since the support/resistance level formed.

■ If a new daily level forms that day, but *does not* hold for a total of 10 days, that level *can still be used* for a swing trade later, when it does hold for 10 consecutive days at that daily level H/L.

This is very tricky to express. In my program I literally *show* you on real-time charts. All I can offer here is a simple screenshot (see Figure 5.1) that reveals a swing level that just formed.

You can see how the most recent 10 trading sessions held above the 185.59 daily support level. This made the 185.59 daily level become a first-tier swing support level. So if the current price of 190.08 were to

FIGURE 5.1 Swing Level

drop down on this day, then once the price broke the 185.59 first-tier swing level I would have a swing *long* position.

■ How to Determine the First-Tier Swing Level

After you scrutinize the *daily* candlestick chart, and you search for pre-established daily levels that have held for *10 consecutive* trading sessions, that's when you determine the *first-tier* swing price level.

"What is a first tier?" you may ask. *Tier* is my term for each swing price level. Don't confuse this with the *intra-day three-tier setups* that I taught you in Part 2. When I use the word *tier* here, I'm strictly speaking of daily price levels that have specifically become swing levels. So, in essence, a swing tier is simply a daily price level that has held for 10 days or more.

The key, and the absolute challenge, is to find the *first* swing support/resistance level. That price level is your *first tier*. The most challenging part of this system is to know when a swing tier has cycled through, meaning it's already hit and profited, or in some cases passed over due to overnight gaps.

For instance, let's say you have a first-tier swing entry at 195.00 (resistance—short trade), and a second-tier swing entry at 198.00 (resistance). In this scenario you'd be shorting soon after they each break. But here's the difficult part: suppose the 195.00 tier breaks and then pulls back for a profit—then what do you do? This means that your second tier at 198.00 now becomes a first-tier swing level (short trade).

This will make more sense later. For now, just know that tiers are constantly changing, and if you're not on top of them, then you're probably trading the wrong price level.

> The 5 percent rule: The range from first tier to last tier within 5 percent.

Now that I've shown you the framework of the 10-day hold rule in swing, and I've introduced you to first-tier swing levels, you're ready to learn the *within 5 percent rule*. If your price levels are correctly logged on your whiteboard, this rule is pretty straightforward. The same is true if you're in my training program, where I have them already logged for you in my online trading room.

"What is this 5 percent rule?" Essentially it states that once you determine your *first-tier swing price level*, then you need to know all the swing price levels that follow. Whether those levels are swing supports or resistance, either way the 5 percent rule applies.

For instance, suppose you have a *first-tier swing support price level* at 187.05. All you need to do is take *5 percent* of that number and *subtract* the amount from the first-tier number (as in *subtract* when swing levels are supports, and *add* when they're at resistance).

In the example in Figure 5.2 you'd have approximately 177.00 as your low end of the 5 percent range.

I say "range" because I'm trying to find all the swing levels that are within a 5 percent *range* of the first swing entry.

In this illustration you have five swing tiers to trade. Later I show the framework of how you trade these tiers. For now I'm just showing you the basics.

This chart is a sample from my online trading room. It shows how the 5 percent rule is applied. Note that the final swing support (daily *low* level) is 176.62. That number is slightly outside of 5 percent (38 cents lower). In some cases this is allowed. There are several reasons why, but here I'll offer just a couple of reasons that will make perfect sense to you. They will also shed light on the fact

Stock: GS ---------- Earnings: APRIL 15- AM

NOTES:

Daily HIGH Levels		Daily LOW Levels	
DATE	PRICE LEVEL	DATE	PRICE LEVEL
5/2/2008****	203.39		
12/8/2014	198.06		
10/14/09****	193.6		
10/6/2014	189.5	2/20/2015	187.05
1/23/2015	182.98	12/1/2014	185.59
1/15/2014	179.74	12/16/2014	182.4
		10/1/2014	180.33
		9/9/2014	176.62
7/30/2014	177.48	10/16/2014	171.26

1st tier

5%

FIGURE 5.2 GS Earnings

that, as I've mentioned before, you need to trade every stock differently.

This stock is GS. Even though it's a highly priced stock, it's actually one of the stocks that moves relatively slowly compared to my other fast movers, like TSLA and BIDU. This is one reason why I allowed the final tier to be slightly outside of 5 percent.

Whenever I determine the 5 percent range, I typically allow for $1 over or under, but that's *not* a constant rule. In some cases I won't include a level when it's over or under $2, off the 5 percent.

Another reason of many is that the next tier (the sixth swing level at 171.26) is over $5 off. So you see, no decision is across the board. Everything depends on the stock.

For now I can tell you that in most cases, you *don't* trade all five levels (all tiers) simply because they are swing levels. This is the biggest reason why traders try my system and fail. They haphazardly enter off *every* swing level, thinking they will profit on each. That couldn't be farther from the truth.

I deliberately built in some procedures and processes that help you determine which levels to trade. Knowing which level to start at and how many shares to apply to each entry is the most difficult part of this system. Again, you're only looking at a framework of how to attain your *first-tier swing price level*, and certainly not your *swing entry level*. In this early point of my instruction, I feel I should make that very clear.

To reiterate, the 187.05 first-tier swing price level is *not* your first entry when it first breaks—not necessarily. It can be, but recognizing the price level is not the same thing as trading it, and as I said, people not formally taught to trade this system assume they can trade every level.

What they don't know is that if they don't know the price level that works the best for them, this system will not work properly. I'm not saying that the levels are off; I'm saying that certain price levels may work for some, but may not work for others. I touch upon this again later. In Chapter 10, I discuss my trading room and how the swing price levels are traded.

■ Understanding Entry and Exit Setup Rules

Let's focus on the entry/exit portion of my swing trading system. This is strictly a screenshot of how you determine the exact price levels to enter and exit at. Of course the most challenging part is deciding which swing price level (tier) you will trade.

Assuming you've completed all your chart analysis homework, and you've chosen today's swing price level to trade, then all you need to do now is wait for the price to run *past* your swing level by *50 cents to $2*, which depends on several factors.

Note that I refer to the swing levels as *daily* levels in this chart. This is because all swing levels are daily levels, but only certain daily levels can be swing traded.

In Figure 5.3 are the entry rules, with a quick list of what to do with differently priced stocks.

Note that if a stock is priced at or over $250, you'll only be looking for *short* swing trades and you'll need to go a full $2 past. If you're

Entry:

- Initial break of $0.50 past DAILY LEVEL on stocks priced $100-$150.
- Initial break of $1.00 past DAILY LEVEL on stocks priced $150-$250.
- Initial break of $2.00 past DAILY LEVEL on stocks priced over $250. (SHORTS ONLY)

FIGURE 5.3 Entry Rules

a greenhorn, however, and especially if you've never been formally trained, you should simply *stop* trading a stock that's over $250. If you continue trading a stock that starts climbing above $250, you're on a very slippery slope. Great examples of this include AMZN and AAPL (before the split). Even if you go $2 past, these stocks can easily jump $15–$20 in one day and also *not* retrace. So until you have mastered this system, just stay away when over $250.

Next come the exit rules. Those that I've mapped here are very straightforward. I sometimes take more than $2, and I sometimes only take 50 percent of the profit target. I clarify this later.

What I want you to do for now is just remain highly consistent, and that means absolutely no guesswork. This is easier said than done. If I were to ask most novice traders what their exit strategy is, most would have very mixed answers. The right answer is highly consistent, and for good reason.

If you take a $2 profit ($200 on every 100 shares) on a stock priced over $150, that's being very conservative, especially when you've considered that the stock price has most likely already run $20+ in one direction before you entered. The current price is extremely overbought/oversold. Therefore a small $2 pullback is very likely to happen, and soon. It may take all day, and in some cases it may take an entire week, before you receive your $2 profit. But the critical thing to remember is that your profit potential is very high when you take only $2 on each swing entry. Keep in mind, if you have a 4-tier setup, that's a potential of $800 profit when it reverses for $2 pullback on your average price of all four tiers. But let's not get ahead of ourselves.

As for the flipside, you should not be selling yourself short by exiting too soon. I can't tell you how many times I've seen the stock price come within 20 cents of my exit but pull back a full dollar or more—this is normal. But you should always wait for your profit. If you break your consistency, in the long run you'll lose out. *Trust the system and earn your money.* Later I show examples of when you should take less than your normal profit target.

"So why $2 profits?" you might ask. You take $1.50 to $2.00 profits for the same reason that you take exactly 15 cents on intra-day trades—a much higher probability of hitting. Think about it: after a major support/resistance is broken and surpassed, the pullback is very likely to give back 15 cents on intra-day trades and at least $1.50 to $2.00 on swing trades, especially when you're countertrend trading.

Figure 5.4 illuminates the exit price points.

> In some cases you have to exit a trade at *50 percent of your profit target*.

If your current swing position on *one or several tiers* (average price) is *in the green 50 percent or more* at the bell at 3:59 P.M., then you need to take your profits before the bell rings. It's not worth the risk to hold your swing position overnight, not when you're already in the green 50 percent or more of your profit target. The trade is over.

Here's a scenario that will help to clarify the 50 percent profit rule. Suppose you enter a *long* swing position at 185.00. For a $2.00 profit, your profit target would be to exit at 187.00. But it's 3:55 P.M. and the current price is at 186.10. This is a great time to exit at 186.00 or higher. This way you can at least lock in a $1.00+ profit on your swing trade—50 percent of your profit target. Note that the swing tier you were trading and exited at 50 percent profit is no longer a swing level—you need to trade the next tier now.

Exit:

-Take a **$1.50** profit on stocks priced **$100-$150**
-Take a **$2.00** profit on stocks priced **$150-$250**

FIGURE 5.4   Exit Price Points

The 50 percent rule is particularly good for newbies to this system, whether they're greenhorn or advanced. As someone who has mastered this system, I will definitely hold overnight at times, because I'm anticipating much more than a $1.00 profit on the trade. This is especially true during earnings release season (just after the release of earnings). You are a newbie, however, and you should just be thinking about *safety*. This rule is highly conservative, and very wise for beginners to use when trading this system for the first time. Also consider that you may have entered off the wrong level, so any profit over 50 percent of its potential is a great opportunity to exit.

■ Two Key Swing Rules to Follow

These two rules are extremely important and also the most misused and/or disregarded. Even the most advanced traders in my program continue to struggle with these. (They are numbered for quick reference purposes only. Neither is more or less important than the other.)

Rule #1

If the price breaks any *swing tier*, and then comes *within 25 cents* of your *swing entry price,* and then *retraces your $1.50 to 2.00 profit amount* (or more) *before* hitting your swing entry price, you just missed the trade. *Do not enter!* This rule applies no matter what tier you're trading.

For instance, if your first-tier swing level (resistance) is $193.28 and the current price reaches $194.25 (not the full $1.00 past), and then it retraces all the way back down to 192.25 ($2.00 retrace from $194.25 level), then you just missed the swing trade. Figure 5.5 shows this scenario. It's very discouraging when this happens, but better safe than sorry.

Also consider that once your first-tier swing level cycles through that means your second-tier swing level now reverts to being the first tier. The chart in Figure 5.6 helps to clarify this. Note that the 198.06 is currently the second-tier swing resistance, but once the 193.28 level pulled back for a $2 profit, then the 198.06 immediately becomes the new first-tier swing level.

FIGURE 5.5   GS One-Minute Chart

HIGHS RESISTANCE LEVELS	LOWS SUPPORT LEVELS
203.39	177.00
198.06	175.41
193.28	173.72

1st Tier Swing Resistance

FIGURE 5.6   First-Tier Swing Resistance

This rule is critical. If you trade a swing level that's already been traded (or missed), then you risk reentering into a price run, and I promise things will get ugly very fast. This goes for intra-day setups as well.

The best way to avoid this mishap is good old-fashioned due diligence. Back-testing on the one-minute candlestick chart will show whether the price has already retraced and whether the trade is over. This may be hard to digest without my showing you in real time on the charts, so for now just be aware that you may be trading a swing level that is actually no longer a swing level, and back-testing is the solution. You can easily double-check each swing level in five minutes or less, late at night and early in the morning. I do it three to five times each morning, on up to eight stocks, simultaneously. Once you master this system, it will only take you about 15 minutes to spot-check your swing levels on up to 10 stocks, all before the bell rings.

I can guarantee that most traders who attempt this system without formal training will screw this rule up royally. Recall that 90 percent of this system is being in rhythm with your price levels. The key here is to know your stock, and to know its price levels at all times, especially just prior to entering a swing trade. It just takes minutes to double-check, and that's the difference between holding a loser and making a quick $2 profit.

I never said this system is easy. It takes focus and patience and caution to get your correct entry price. You're getting paid for staying on top of your price levels. So earn your pay!

Rule #2

If your *swing level entry price* hits during *pre-market*, then *wait* to make your first entry off the intra-day *pre-market low/high* once the market opens.

For instance, suppose your swing *entry price* is at 179.56 (long), and it hits 179.56 in pre-market trading. You *wait* to trade until *after* the bell rings. Whatever the pre-market *low* is, you enter at *50 cents past*. And that's how, if the pre-market *low* hits 178.82, your swing entry is 178.32 when it *initially* hits, after the bell rings.

This is a great example of how intra-day and swing setups merge. In Part 4, you'll learn more about this. Here I just need you to recognize that pre-market price levels are very important to both intra-day and swing setups. Also keep in mind that in this example, your swing entry of 178.32 and not 179.56 just saved you $1.24 on your trade. It can be viewed as entering your swing trade $1.24 richer.

Also consider this in pre-market trading, as in Rule #1: *if the price hits the swing entry and then profits a full $2 in pre-market, and then the tier is gone, then you trade the next tier.*

■ Buying Power and Trading Experience Dictate Your Swing Strategy

I want to make this very clear. Before you decide which stock(s) to swing trade (priced $100–$250), and before you decide how many shares you will swing trade, you need to consider the amount of *cash/capital* in your brokerage account (your non-leveraged buying power), and you need to consider your level of knowhow with my intra-day and swing systems.

These two factors are the main issues when you determine what swing price level you enter at, and how many shares at each swing tier. In other words, just because a swing level is hitting today, that does *not* mean you should be trading that price level (swing tier), and that does *not* mean you should be going more than 100 shares on each swing level. For instance, with my swing strategy you *don't hold marginalized positions overnight*. Therefore, all your *swing* trades should be purchased with *cash-capital*. This one rule keeps the risk of holding overnight down to a minimum.

According to SEC regulations, you're allowed to hold overnight up to a *2:1 leverage/margin*. But my strategy is fiscally more conservative. By using your own capital you eliminate the largest risk of holding overnight: the dreaded *margin call*.

To recap, the margin call is when you're required to sell enough of your losing positions/shares to get your *capital/margin ratio within the 2:1 leverage*. In other words, if you're holding leverage overnight, you're forced to sell a position if you're in the red *at any point*. This creates an inevitable problem when trading with my system, because, don't forget, you *will* be in the red: this is expected and normal with *swing* trades, but you *won't* want to have to sell a position *prematurely*.

Most pattern-day traders who have a traditional broker will have *at least 25K* in their trading account. This means they can afford to purchase 100 shares of a $250 stock and hold overnight *without* any margin call issues or worries, or, to put it numerically, 200 shares of $125 stock.

The only downside to having limited capital (25K *minimum*) is that you may be holding a swing trade for days and sometimes even weeks.

This means you *cannot* intra-day trade other stocks while you wait on your current swing position to reverse to a profit.

■ Here's the *Good* News!

I have strategies that will help to maximize your chances of entering a swing trade that isn't likely to last more than a few days, and in many cases will reverse for an intra-day profit. One great example is simple: once you know your 5 percent range and have your swing tiers, and you have four price levels within 5 percent, then all you need to do is wait for the third or fourth tier to hit. This way, if you can only afford 200 shares overnight, then only trade the final two tiers.

If you try trading tiers 1 and 2, then you risk the price running against you and not having enough capital to recapture stronger price levels at tiers 3 and 4. You risk having to hold your position much longer if the prices run the full 5 percent. This is a very basic example of trading on minimum capital funds. Again, you need at least 25K to trade this system properly, and any amount of capital between 25 and 50K would be considered minimum capital. This is not just true for my system, but for all *real* day trading systems.

As you can imagine, most Wall Street day traders are highly capitalized and not worried about these restrictions, so they tend to trade every swing tier, and with much more than 100 shares per price level entered. For you, however, capital is one big restriction, and another is your trading experience level. The amount of knowhow you have with this system will dictate which tiers you should trade and which tiers you should avoid. Every beginner in my program starts by *avoiding all first-tier* swing levels.

"Why?" First tiers are the most risky, the low end of the 5 percent range. They can run 5 percent against you, and you don't have enough capital to capture the stronger levels. After you see the entire framework, all this will make more sense.

> Whether you have *100* shares or *1,000*, you take *the same amount of profits*.

This rule can't be overemphasized. In most cases you'll take the same amount of profit, no matter how many shares. This is generally true in the 100- to 1,000-share range. This rule changes when you get over 1,000 shares per position. However, 99 percent of traders are *not* going to trade in 1,000-share block trades. More typically, many of my advanced trainees quickly start trading in 200-share block trades and still capture their $2 profit target.

Here I have mapped out the framework of my swing trading system. In Chapter 6, I show several sample charts to clarify the swing system visually.

## CHAPTER 6

Sample Swing Charting Setups

This chapter showcases some very helpful charts. They're all about swing trading setups. These setups are actual historical trades and all of them can be back-tested.

Keep in mind that some of the swing levels hit in pre-market, and therefore they were skipped. You can't see pre-market data on a daily candlestick chart. This is one more reason why it's critical that you stay on top of your swing levels every day and are watching to see if levels hit in pre-market. I assure you that this is one of the top 10 reasons why non-formally trained traders misuse this system.

In Part 4, I provide more charts to help mold a solid understanding of how this system works. In Part 3, however, you only need to focus on the basics: (1) the 5 percent rule and (2) the 10-day hold rule. Basically, you need to focus on swing setups exclusively.

You may notice that several of the chart examples date back to 2012. Their age makes absolutely no difference. The rules and procedures that applied then apply just as much to this day. I purposefully chose older chart setups in order to prove that point.

Looking over Figure 6.1, you can see that the 151.97 *daily level* (resistance) *held* for 10 days, making it your first-tier swing, and you can see that you have several higher resistances all within 5 percent of it. Note that the current price on September 12, 2012, opens just

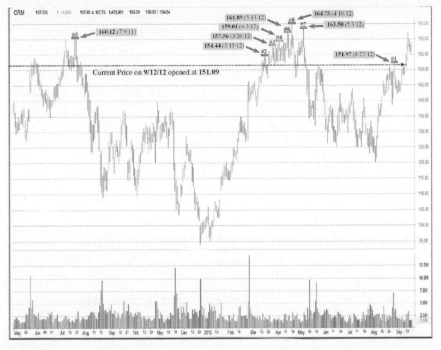

Current Price on 9/12/12 opened at 151.09

FIGURE 6.1 Daily Levels

under the 151.97 first-tier swing level. This price is the first of several swing levels above it, but 151.97 is your first-tier swing on this day.

Depending on your capital buying power and your degree of experience, it may or may not be wise for you to start off at tier #1 (151.97). For now you just need to grasp the process. For convenience we'll assume you can trade all swing levels, including the risky first tier.

In this example you have three other resistance levels *within $7.50 (or within 5%) of the #1—$151.97 (08/27/12) level*. They are:

#2: 154.44 (3/15/12)
#3: 157.56 (3/26/12)
#4: 159.01 (4/03/12)

Note that all the swing levels (daily levels) are more than $1 apart. I chose this particular setup because it's fairly easy to see all of them in one area. Such is not always the case. You can have swing levels that are months apart. A great example is the #5 swing level way back in 2011. All that matters is they're *real* daily levels and fit my criteria for trading.

Note also that they're in numerical order. In this case the numbers are ascending because the price is heading upward to resistance.

You have *four total swing levels* that can be traded, and gain the *full profit target of $2.00 on any one level*. If you happen to accumulate all four levels, then you have a 400-share position and a chance to profit $800 when the *average price* pulls back $2.

■ The 5 Percent Bubble

At this point you might want to know: "What about the levels outside or above the final swing tier in this 5 percent range?"

That is a good question. The answer is you can trade them as well. But what if you don't have the capital to absorb them? That's quite a quandary!

Later I show you several examples of what to do when the price runs past the 5 percent tier. For now, you should focus on two things. The first thing you read in Chapter 5, and I just implied it again, is you will *not* be trading the first tier in any swing trade setup until you master the system. Second, while you're still learning the system, but you know the price can easily break through all levels, you need *not* assume the price will retrace for your $2 profit, not *before* the next swing tier *outside* the 5 percent bubble. And that's an example of how hard it is to explain, only here on paper, which levels work best for the individual trader.

Another hard lesson to teach on paper: be prepared to be holding your swing position while in the red, which could be a day or could be a couple weeks. Being *initially* in the red is a normal process of day trading this system. Again, a classic error in the average amateur trading mindset is they think every trade should immediately go into the green shortly after their first entry. That couldn't be further from reality.

For the sake of helping you learn the basics, I've listed those price levels outside the 5 percent bubble (5% range). I would show #5 in red because that's the *red-zone* tier—outside of 5 percent range.

I'm showing the red zone to prove the point that you'll always have higher levels to trade outside of 5 percent. If you didn't, this system would be bogus. On all swing trade levels, you certainly do run the risk of running far past the 5 percent. In this case you have several swing price levels past 159.01.

Keep this in mind: the 5 percent swing range is *after* the price is *already way overbought*. Therefore, it's highly unlikely that the price will run past the 5 percent range *before* it reverses back for your $1.50 to $2.00 profit. And even if that happens, I have rules and strategies to adjust your swing trade so it ultimately results in a profit.

Stay tuned. And hang in there. I know this is rough, like doing a 500-piece jigsaw puzzle in your head without any pieces in your hands. I warned you about the map not being the road.

The red tier is the first swing level *outside* the 5 percent bubble:

#8: 164.75 (4/19/12)
#7: 163.50 (5/03/12)
#6: 161.89 (4/13/12)
#5: 160.12 (7/19/11)

When you take in both of the charts (in Figures 6.1 and 6.2), the first thing to notice is that each is a *daily* chart of the stock CRM. This is SalesForce.com *before* the split. Each is the same time frame and price levels, except one shows the *daily levels* (Figure 6.1) and the other shows the *entry points* for swing trades (Figure 6.2).

Beginning with Figure 6.2, focus on the area that reads "current price on 09/12/12, opened at 151.09." I determined my swing setups on that date. Leading up to that day, I had acquired several previous *daily* levels. All of them are listed on both charts. I found all those levels according to the guidelines I've previously shown you.

As soon as I knew all my daily levels, I could do some simple math. My first entry was off #1, the 151.97 daily level that formed back on 08/27/12. I noted that this price level hadn't been broken in *less* than 10 days. I also noticed that I had three other daily levels all within 5 percent of my 151.97 price level, and I had a few more just outside my 5 percent range. That made this a *multi-tier swing* trade, meaning I had more than one swing level within 5 percent.

Most swing setups will in fact have multi-tier possibilities. But typically, the only time you'll have one single tier is when the swing level is the all-time high, no tiers after that.

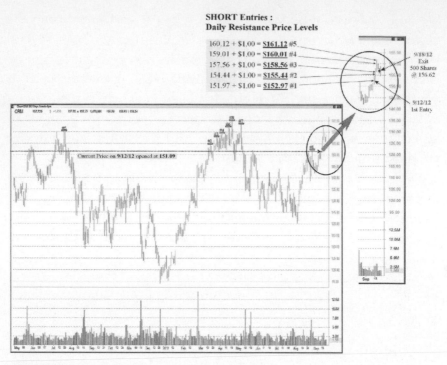

SHORT Entries :
Daily Resistance Price Levels

160.12 + $1.00 = **$161.12** #5
159.01 + $1.00 = **$160.01** #4
157.56 + $1.00 = **$158.56** #3
154.44 + $1.00 = **$155.44** #2
151.97 + $1.00 = **$152.97** #1

9/18/12
Exit
500 Shares
@ 156.62

9/12/12
1st Entry

Current Price on 9/12/12 opened at **151.09**

FIGURE 6.2   Entry Points for Swing Trades

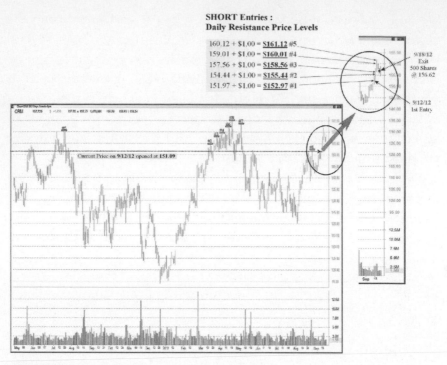

128

SAMPLE SWING CHARTING SETUPS

Even though I've instructed you to *not* trade a first-tier swing price level, it's *critical* that you know where it is and whether it's still in play, meaning not yet reversed for a $2 profit.

Once I establish my first-tier swing level, I average into each and every level above it. But that's *if and only if* I'm prepared to enter at *every single* swing level within the 5 percent bubble, and even outside if it hits.

When it comes to the people I'm training hands-on, funding and experience are the key factors here. I initially have the low-funded trainees only trade the final tier, and I do the same with the trainees who are struggling with mastery. The reading of this manual is a limited, very one-dimensional encounter with my training technique. Just make sure you know this:

> You *do not* trade every single swing tier simply because the price levels hit.

■ Swing Trade Setups

I'm finished doling out cautionary advice for the moment. Now I'll show you this setup. On September 12, 2012, I placed a first 100-share *short* trade at 152.97. It closed at 152.71, slightly in the green (26 cents). It was *not* more than 50 percent of my profit target of $2.00, so I *held* overnight (recall the 50% profit-taking rule that I discussed in Chapter 5).

On September 13, 2012, the price ran toward the next higher daily levels, before retracing to my $2.00 profit target price of 150.97. When it hit the next daily level of 154.44 and $1.00 past that level, I entered *my second 100-share swing trade at 155.44*. Once again the price ran against me and closed in the red, so *I held 200 shares overnight*.

On September 14, 2012, the price reached an intra-day high of 161.90 during the first hour of trading. So I was able to grab my third and fourth swing trade off the 157.56 and 159.01 daily levels, $1.00 past. Note that these two levels were both within the 5 percent range. But the price reached the 160.12 daily level and went $1.00 past that level, so I entered my fifth 100-share swing trade at 161.12. This level placed my entry *outside* of the 5 percent range, meaning I would have to *cut my profit limit in half*. Instead of a $2.00 gain (from the average price), I would now look to exit all 500 shares at a $1.00 average profit.

This constitutes an *addition* to the 50 percent profit rule: if a swing runs past the 5 percent range, then you only take 50 percent of your profit, as I did in this case when I took $1.00.

My *average* on all five trades (500 shares) was $157.62. So the thing for me to do was to *hold* this until it went down to 156.62, or else *short* for another 100 shares if it continued up to the next daily level on May 13, 2012, at 161.89, entering the sixth position at 162.89.

Because this price run was extremely overbought, and my swing entry levels were each *real* price levels drawn from the daily chart, the price ultimately ran back down. It took *five* trading sessions to swing this trade into the green. A couple of days after my last entry, on September 18, 2012, I exited all 500 shares when it hit 156.62; that was a $500 profit.

You need 80K in buying capital to make that happen. That's 500 shares times the average cost of 157.62. If you had only *25K*, then you would have only been able to *hold 200 shares overnight*, with little or no margin. You would have waited for the *highest* price in the 5 percent range to hit. You would have entered 100 shares at $160.01 on September 12, 2012, off the #4 swing level of 159.01 on April 2, 2012. You would have held it for a few hours that day to gain a $2.00 profit, or a $200 share profit when it hit at $158.01.

This is a great example of how having limited capital isn't so bad. You simply wait for the strongest swing levels to hit—get in last minute on multi-tier swings. Just keep in mind that if this is your strategy, you need to be aware that if all the previous swing levels (in this case lower resistance levels) hit and then reversed for $2 profit, then your 159.01 fourth-tier swing would have become first tier. Beware! This will make more sense later.

Figures 6.3 and 6.4 show setups for IBM. Again I have a *multi-tier* setup, or *short* position. But in these examples I show different options for which levels to enter, depending on what you have for trading capital. These setups are more involved. They're a great example of how certain older swing levels can get trumped by newly forming ones.

Notice in Figure 6.4 that the day I entered the first *swing short* was on September 11, 2012, and the opening price that day was 200.55.

Notice the *five daily* resistance levels:

#1: 202.00 (8/17/12)
#2: 207.52 (3/16/12)*—drops off
#3: 207.99 (5/03/12)*
#4: 208.93 (5/1/12)*
#5: 210.69 (9/13/12)

---

*I've asterisked the daily levels #2, #3, and # 4 because the 207.52 level got replaced by the 207.99 (within $1.00 of each other). The 207.99 and the 208.93 swing levels were also within $1.00, but I allowed the 207.99 level to remain because the 207.99 trumped the 207.52, almost one full dollar. I swing traded the 207.99.

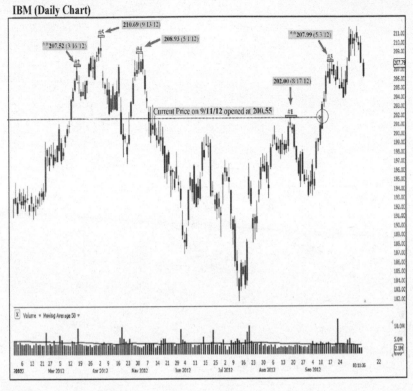

IBM (Daily Chart)

210.69 (9/13/12)

#5

**207.52 (3/16/12)

208.93 (5/1/12)

**207.99 (5/3/12)

#2

#4

#3

202.00 (8/17/12)

Current Price on 9/11/12 opened at 200.55

#1

Volume ▾ Moving Average 50 ▾

6 13 21 27 5 12 19 26 2 9 16 23 30 7 14 21 29 4 11 18 25 2 9 16 23 30 6 13 20 27 4 10 17 24 02:11:36 22
2022   Mar 2012   Apr 2012   May 2012   Jun 2012   Jul 2012   Aug 2012   Sep 2012

FIGURE 6.3 IBM Setup

You might ask: "Once you have your levels to swing trade, which ones should you trade first?" The four levels are within 5 percent of each other, from #1 to #5 (202.00–210.69). That means they all can be traded. But what if this was your trade? You might not be able to afford all the levels. If you could afford to purchase all four, then you'd start with the first at 202.00.

Figure 6.4 represents how I traded a 400-share swing setup. You should study it with the assumption that you can afford up to 400 shares of this $200 stock. After this example I show other options for when you have limited capital, like trading with 50K.

I placed my first swing *short* on September 11, 2012, when the price hit 203.00. It never retraced for a $2.00 profit, so I *held* overnight. The next entry wasn't for about two weeks, when it *broke* the 207.99 *daily* level (new level) on October 1, 2012. That was when I entered

FIGURE 6.4 IBM 400-Share Swing Setup

my second swing *short* at 208.99. Yes, you read that right: I said *two weeks!*

Let this be a reminder that some first-tier swings can take weeks before pullback. This is one more reason why if you're trading with limited capital, you should not touch a first-tier swing entry. You run the risk of your minimal funding being tied up for days, if not weeks.

Now back to the trade setup. On the same day (10/1/12), it happened to also break the next two levels. So I entered at 209.93 and 211.69.

> *Fact:* The *average price* of all 400 swing entries is $208.40.

All I needed to do now was take my average price on 400 shares and sell when it retraced $2.00 on the average price. So I waited for $206.40 to hit and it did a week later, on October 10, 2012.

In summary, this trade from start to finish took about one month to make an $800 profit. This is fine when you have enough capital to trade other stocks while waiting this one out.

Figure 6.5 exemplifies how to swing trade when you have limited capital.

This chart shows my first trade was off the 207.99 *daily* level (second-tier swing price level), and not the 202.00 first-tier swing level.

"Why is this?" you might ask. Because in the Figure 6.4 example, all four levels were *within* 5 percent, so I went with the first level at 202.00 because I had enough capital to average into all four.

But never forget that without high funds or much experience, you want to start your entry with the second, third, fourth, or final level—in accordance with what you have. If you can only afford

FIGURE 6.5 Swing Trade with Limited Capital

100 shares, then you wait for the 210.69 level to hit. Or if you have enough for 300 shares, then you trade as Figure 6.5 suggests. Either way, you make a profit.

Figures 6.6 and 6.7 show setups for BIDU. Again I have a *multi-tier* setup within a 5 percent bubble. This time it's a *long* trade. This setup also shows how I traded off the *pre-market* levels (recall the entry swing rule).

Notice the current day is October 8, 2012, and the price opened at 113.08. At that point I had three *daily* levels that could be swing traded. Note the huge gap-down overnight. I was waiting for the #1 daily level to swing trade, but it never broke until the gap-down, so the price finally hit in pre-market.

FIGURE 6.6   BIDU Setup

FIGURE 6.7 BIDU Long Entries

Below are the three daily price levels that I had at the time of the gap-down. But at no point was the entry prior to the gap-down.

110.06
107.50
106.60

Note that 107.50 and 106.60 are *less than $1.00 apart*. This is allowed when the price of the stock is so close to the minimum of $100, but I *never* allow less than *75 cents apart*.

On the next day, October 9, 2012, the price opened at 109.04, *but the price hit a low of 108.82 in pre-market*. According to the *entry* swing rules, I needed to enter my first swing trade as an intra-day

FIGURE 6.8 Log Sheet

trade, off the pre-market level. In this case, the pre-market low was 108.82, so I entered first *long* swing entry trade at 108.32 (50 cents past 108.32), and this was soon after the bell rang.

Note that I entered the *initial* time it hit 108.32 on October 9, 2012. The price continued to drop on the same day, so I entered *50 cents past* the next two swing levels (107.50 and 106.60).

In Figure 6.7, I blew up the area showing the profit. You'll notice that I had to *hold* all 300 shares overnight. The price on October 10, 2012, retraced $1.50, on average. I profited $450 on this trade.

Figure 6.8 is a snapshot of the log sheet in my swing trading room. This is how I log my swing trades. You should use the same layout and information when you practice.

You've seen the basic framework of my swing trading strategy. You have a better understanding of the rules and procedures for both my intra-day and swing trading methodologies. Now you're ready to tackle the fusion of both: Fusion Trading.

## PART IV

The *Fusion* of Intra-Day and Swing Strategies

## CHAPTER 7

Introduction to Fusion Trading

The term *Fusion Trading* is my own. I like to use that term for quick reference. You'll see it here over and over, and my trainees hear me say it all the time. But you won't find it listed on Wikipedia—not yet. And for now, you won't hear the word *fusion* on Wall Street unless you bump into one of my graduates.

Though the term is my invention, the system itself is not. Fusion is creatively implemented by most professional day traders, especially the countertrend traders. As a whole, fusion methodology gives trading on Wall Street the legendary calibre it's known for. The more you get acquainted with this system, the more you're going to realize that the same key price levels that I trade are traded in high volume on Wall Street. Now that you've seen both my intra-day and swing trading frameworks, this part of the text will make perfect sense to you (about as much sense as a map makes without your having been on the road).

Before I get straight to the core of fusion trading, I want to point out a couple of facts. Most novices call themselves either "intra-day" or "swing" traders without a full understanding of how each distinct strategy works. Some jump right to swing trading (*ouch!*), and some never advance from intra-day trading to mastery of the swing setups.

As I've mentioned many times previously, fusion is the synergy of both, and you're going to find that my use of both strategies for every trade setup (yes, I said *every* trade setup) is totally logical. The reason is that intra-day and swing methods are *not* mutually exclusive.

■ Why Are They Not Mutually Exclusive?

Most beginners try to learn day trading alone, and advanced traders tend to be lone wolves who came up the hard way without much help, showcasing the scars from their disasters. The novices tend to be unaware that the full scope means using both systems, and even the much more experienced, who know something about orchestrating fusion, fail to achieve consistent profits.

No matter whether they're beginners or not, very few traders come to me knowing these critical facts:

- Intra-day trading must be learned prior to swing trading.
- Intra-day and swing trading are very much interlinked (Fusion Trading).

When I first started trading in 1998, nobody taught me those two facts. With regard to the first fact, I hadn't been properly coached. The professional trading seminars and workshops I attended never taught me that truth. I did learn how to read charts, both the intra-day and the dailies. I got a good sense of what an intra-day price level is, and what is a stronger swing level. But I was never taught how to differentiate them, or to start *first* with intra-day setups.

As a result, I would mistakenly trade an intra-day support/ resistances level. And then, if my trade was in the red at market close, I would always *hold overnight*. I thought that was okay.

That was a classic mistake! I wasn't fully cognizant that the intra-day levels I traded were not strong enough to hold past that day. Now I know different, and I emphatically teach it. Not only is that type of overnight hold as risky as hanging off a cliff by your thumb, it doesn't even make sense to do it. Think about it. Why would you do this with a weak intra-day level when you're only supposed to be profiting 15 cents on it?

But many novice traders simply hold overnight and pray that the stock price goes in their favor by the next market opening. Does the "slippery slope" image come to mind here? It should.

There are logical reasons why the mastery of intra-day *first* makes perfect sense. Most importantly, when you start to learn trading, it's imperative that you remain in a low-risk exposure environment. Only the intra-day setups provide that safety net. If you've been instructed to minimize risk, then you know to not hold overnight, and you're looking for quick exits. On the contrary, swing trades are held for much longer and usually with more shares. So putting off the learning of swing trades and starting with intra-day setups is a great way to get to know your stock without losing your shirt in the process.

This process cannot be fast-tracked!

Parts 1 through 3 made you very aware that whether you're intra-day or swing trading, you need to know your pre-market data, and you need to know how to read a one-minute candlestick chart (just to name a couple of essentials). You also learned that mastery of intra-day trading is prerequisite to your swing setups.

The ultimate reason to start with intra-day trading is all about what I call the *rhythm factor*. I've alluded to this before. This is about profoundly reading your stock, just as you do with every nuance of your all-time-favorite song, just as profoundly as you read your life partner. The rhythm factor is working when you know your stocks inside and out, and you master this feat only with an intra-day trading foundation.

Even I, the founder of this system, cannot start swing trading a new stock without watching and getting in rhythm with it on an intra-day basis first. This process can take weeks and even months. I want to know how my new stock trades in pre-market. I want to know how it trades when it's breaking daily price levels (for both intra-day and swing setups). I'm all over it: intra-day price movements, the speed, the average H/L range per day, and so on.

I need to get in rhythm with my new stocks because eventually I'm going to marry them. I can't be that guy who's planning his wedding while he's driving to his blind date! Back when I was a novice, every time I didn't commit to learning a stock's total rhythm, things ended very ugly. I learned the hard way.

Here you can learn from my mistakes. I've mapped out a golden path. Just stay on the path; don't meander. Stick with the sequence of intra-day first, and then get into swing, and then the fusion of both.

Guess what? You can't trade intra-day without knowing your swing levels.

"*What?*" I can picture you yelling. I just taught you to start with intra-day first. So what's that conundrum about?

It's critical to learn the *entire* system *prior* to trading *live* with real money. I'm not saying you can't intra-day trade exclusively. Sure you can. But either way, you need to know where your swing levels are prior to entering an intra-day setup.

Here's an example of why you need to know both at once. Suppose you wanted to enter an intra-day trade without knowing where your next swing tier was at. You could be as much as $10+ off your mark. This is why, in Part 2, I had you practice the Golden Rules. Remember the rule that commands you to only enter an intra-day trade if it's *within $3 of a daily price level*? You're going to find in this part of the book that those *daily levels can become swing levels*.

Consider this. If you were to find strong swing levels, but you failed to account for newly formed intra-day levels, such as pre-market intra-day levels, then your swing entry would be off the mark on virtually every trade. Any system that shows you strong swing levels and has you place static entries the next day *without* accounting for newly formed intra-day levels is a system that's going to fail.

Let's take a look at the system in action. I'll begin with the basics and show a sample trade setup to help you understand visually how this works.

Your goal in fusing both strategies is to plan your intra-day trades in conjunction with your swing setups. That's precisely why you must know your swing levels *prior* to entering any intra-day setup, and vice-versa. Using my Golden Rules, you must know your intra-day setups in order to trade into a swing. Yes, you'll learn intra-day trading first, but ultimately in every trade with this system you're going to *initially* define the trade by the swing levels/tiers.

> Here's a rule of thumb: *you will enter your intra-day trade within $3 of a swing entry*. No swing level, no intra-day trade — it's that simple!

Figure 7.1 shows a classic fusion trade setup using LNKD.

Suppose you had a first-tier swing *long* level at 173.72. You would wait to start intra-day trading until the *intra-day support price levels* formed in the range of $176.00–$177.00 (within $3 of your first-tier *swing* level). Once you entered the first intra-day trade, and *if* the price ran against you, then you could enter again off your *swing* level.

Below I address three primary guidelines and procedures that clarify how you capture all these levels on Figure 7.1. It boils down to these key intra-day and swing trade setup-preparations:

1. You need to know where your first-tier swing level is.
2. You need to be armed with your *prior price levels* on your whiteboard by 9:30 A.M., with the numbers in numerical order.
3. You apply the Golden Rules once the bell rings.

The charts in Figures 7.2 and 7.3 show the *prior* price levels that were gathered on LNKD during pre-market on April 4, 2014.

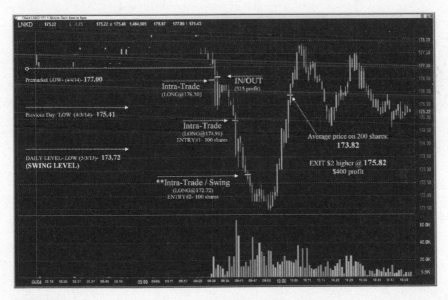

FIGURE 7.1   Classic Fusion Trade Setup

PRIOR PRICE LEVELS

		Stock:	LNKD				
Pre market			Previous Day			Daily H/L	
Date:	4/4/2014	Date:	4/3/2014		HIGH	LOW	
HIGH	178.30	HIGH	183.33		183.87.	173.72	
LOW	177.00	LOW	175.41				

FIGURE 7.2   Prior Price Levels—LNKD

HIGHS RESISTANCE LEVELS	LOWS SUPPORT LEVELS
183.87	177.00
183.33	175.41
178.30	173.72

1st Tier Swing Support

FIGURE 7.3   First-Tier Swing Support Level

■ Applying the Golden Rules

To keep things basic for now, I've simply shown you the *first-tier swing support level*, which is 173.72. If you were to back-test, you'd find that, according to the swing rules and procedures in Part 3, at that time it was in fact a first-tier swing level.

For your convenience, in Figure 7.2, I've listed all the *prior* levels that pertain to the trade setup in Figure 7.1. I also created the *whiteboard* chart in Figure 7.3, which takes all the numbers from Figure 7.2 and puts them in numerical order.

As you know from your previous reading, the final step in the process is applying the Golden Rules. You can enter your first trade after the bell rings, *if* the Rules indicate you should. The Rules are so important that I'm displaying them again here in a feature box for reference.

Intra-Day Golden Rules (Recap)

Rule No. 1: Always know your second entry before you enter your first trade.

Rule No. 2: On all your initial trade setups, you must have at least one daily price level with $3 of your first entry. If not, then no initial trade.

Rule No. 3: You must have a maximum of three tiers for each trade setup (300 shares).

Rule No. 4: Your initial entry (first 100 shares) can be off any intra-day high/low or any prior level.

Rule No. 5: Never have two entries within 50 cents of each other.

Rule No. 6: When intra-day trading, your entry price will always be a static 25 or 50 cents past your chosen support/resistance level:

- 25 cents past intra-day high/low levels
- 50 cents past prior levels

All levels are 50 cents past up to 9:45 A.M. (the first 15 minutes of trading).

Referring back to Figure 7.1, I will narrate a description of the entire illustrated setup.

It's almost 9:30 A.M. The bell is about to ring. I'm prepared to fusion-trade LNKD because I've found that it's been trading within $3 of the 173.72 first-tier swing price level. I've gathered all my prior price levels and I have them in front of me, looming large across the whiteboard on my wall. I'm locked and loaded and ready to execute a trade—but only if the price drops.

"Why?" you might ask. "You can only intra-day trade if the price *drops?*"

Yes. Think about it. If your first tier is a *support* level, then the price must drop to hit it. Therefore, you're only monitoring your *support* price levels (the right-column numbers in Figure 7.2). In this example the price does drop, so I'll be trading the right-column support levels on the way down.

"What if it shot up instead?" Then there simply would be *no trade*. I'd trade other stocks that day. But chances are whenever I get to within $3 of a swing level, the price does continue in that direction, just as it's doing today.

So here we go! *Ding-ding-ding!* The market is open and the price is plummeting. I have a plan and my price levels to enter at, so execution of the order entry is all I need to do. I apply the Golden Rules for intra-day trading and confirm that the *177.00 support level* can be traded as my *first* entry. Also according to the Rules, 177.00 can be traded because the second entry of 175.41 is within $3 of it, plus my swing level is within $3 of the 177.00 level.

Now all I have to do is wait for the 177.00 price level to break the *initial* time, and then enter the trade at exactly *50 cents past*. Once the price hits 177.00, I enter using fastkey order execution to *buy/long at 176.50*. The order fills very quickly, within minutes after the bell.

What about my *exit strategy?* What profit do I take, *15 cents or $2.00?* I can choose either option. In this example I take the standard 15-cent profit on this intra-day setup. The price pulls back one minute later for my *15-cent profit ($15 profit with 100 shares)*. The trade for 177.00 is over, and now I'm back on the sidelines looking to reenter a new trade at lower price levels.

My next intra-day support price level is 175.41. Can I trade this price level? Yes, it, too, is within $3 of my next entry, because it happens to be the swing price level of 173.72.

About six minutes after my last trade exit, the price continues to drop. At this point, I'm simply waiting for the 175.41 support price level to hit. As soon as it does, I'll execute a *buy/long* limit order for 174.91(50 cents past 175.41).

But this particular intra-day trade doesn't pull back for a 15-cent profit. It continues to drop instead, and it's heading right for my swing price of 173.72. So I make the decision to delete my 15-cent profit target order on the 174.91 entry (intra-day trade), and I prepare to enter my second entry on this new trade setup. But this time the second entry will be a swing entry, so I can hold the entire trade (200 shares) for a full $2 profit.

This trade is about to become a *fusion trade*. It hits the 173.72 swing price level, so I execute another 100-share order at *$1.00 past* 173.72. A couple of minutes later, the price hits 172.72. I now have *200 shares* with an average price of *173.82*. I execute a *sell order for 200 shares at a $2.00 profit*. My exit price target is 175.82. That price hits 15 minutes later and I exit the fusion trade with a *$400 profit*.

Keep in mind that this example reversed on the first-tier swing before the market closed. In many cases the price will run much lower all day, and that's fine, because you'll always have lower swing tiers to enter at. Don't assume the trade will immediately reverse back to the green on the same day, as it does in this example. That's a very common amateur mistake.

> You need to get comfortable with being in the red.

Whenever you're countertrend trading, being in the red is perfectly normal. If you execute your swing levels properly, then you'll always land square in the green.

You might ask: "What if the price never reverses before the market close?"

That's a great question. For now, I'll give the most basic answer. In the example I've shown here, I had 200 shares. One of the trades was a swing trade and the other was an intra-day trade. The first 100-share entry of 174.91 was from an intra-day level. So, if the price didn't hit my $2 profit target on the fusion trade before the close (the 50% profit rule applies here as well), I would have had to sell/close 100 shares at 3:59 P.M. It didn't matter whether that 100 shares was a loss or a profit. You know that I couldn't hold an intra-day position overnight.

I would regain the small loss over the next day, or days, when I would sell my swing position at a $200+ profit. I say $200 *plus* because I could accumulate more swing levels and place more intra-day trades while still in the current swing, thus more potential profits. Also, the price could have gapped up overnight more than $2.

In Part 5, Chapter 9, I introduce what I call *pivot trading* and other advanced strategies. They show you how to recoup losses from intra-day setups that were closed out in the red, before the market closed. For now, just focus on the concept of fusion. You can turn your intra-day setups into a swing and ride them for the full $2 profit. That's all you need to understand at this point.

■ Deciding Your Trading Options: Intra-Day Only, Swing Only, or Fusion?

I *never* use intra-day trading exclusively for 15-cent profits—not anymore.

"Why not?" you might ask. There are a few reasons. The biggest reason is obvious. I would much rather make $2.00 per trade than 15 cents. So would you.

A second reason is I've become a master swing trader. Every trade I make is built around strong swing levels, whether I'm exclusively waiting for a swing level to hit, or I'm fusion trading. Either way, on every trade I'm going to make my profit target of $2. At this point in my trading career, I have no incentive to work hard for intra-day setups, because they net so much less reward. For instance, if my intra-day setup runs deep into the red and the market is about to close, I have no choice but to stop-loss. From time to time this happens to everyone: most of those small profits get wiped out on bad days when the price runs deep into red.

(But as you know, I always use intra-day setups to help determine my swing setups. I'm not looking for intra-day 15-cent profits, but at all times I do watch the intra-day levels while I'm swing and fusion trading.)

Of course you want to learn how to swing trade, for all of the reasons I do, with the goal of exclusively swing trading and/or fusion trading in the future. But you have to start somewhere, and intra-day trading is the place. I dedicate the first two or three weeks of my training program to intra-day trading only, all on a demo trading platform. That way no one loses money, but everyone learns the intra-day system prior to the swing trading system, and at zero monetary risk.

With that said, I now address those who are itching to finish this book and jump right into swing trading without mastering intra-day first.

> You are not yet a master of this system. It takes weeks to learn this system.

So start with intra-day setups and be happy with 15 cents on your trades while practicing on a demo. If you don't, you're going to lose money. Every single trainee who enters my coaching program starts with intra-day trading, and only on harmless demos. After you've mastered the intra-day setups and are in rhythm with your stock(s), then it's time to start the swing trading. Once you master the swing, then you can work on the fusion. You build your skill set to the pinnacle.

Your comfort zone should totally jive with how well you know this system. So should your capital/buying power. For instance, if you have limited capital, you may only want to swing trade, and only trade the strongest swing tiers within the 5 percent bubble (see Part 3). On the other hand, if you're highly capitalized and have mastered both intra-day and swing setups, then you can go right into fusion, and with more than 100 shares per entry.

The sky is the limit when you trade with this system. But I can't possibly know how to coach you without knowing you and your skill set. In this book I can only offer options and leave it to you to decide what works best.

In Chapter 8, I offer several examples of swing setups and fusion setups.

## CHAPTER 8

Sample Fusion Trade Setups

In this chapter I show three classic fusion trade setups that cover the framework of my method. In the following part you'll view several advanced strategies that build upon what you learn here. Here you'll find two sample whiteboards, as charts. They are the standard for *support* or *resistance* fusion trading. I'll be using this whiteboard format from this point on.

Notice that the whiteboard chart in Figure 8.1 includes the *prior* price levels shown in Figure 8.2: *pre-market* and *previous day*. Because you're now learning the full fusion system, the whiteboard will only include the daily levels that are currently swing levels. Also note that I only show the support or resistance levels. This is because on the morning of a possible fusion trade, your focus should be *only* on those levels.

Why is this? Think about it. If a swing level is hitting, it can only be one of those. You will *never* have both a swing support level and swing resistance level hitting on the same day. The only time this could ever happen would be on earnings release dates, and you would *not* be trading until *after* the release, which would typically be the next day.

Once you master this system you'll know before the market opens whether you're trading *long* or *short* on all your trades for any particular

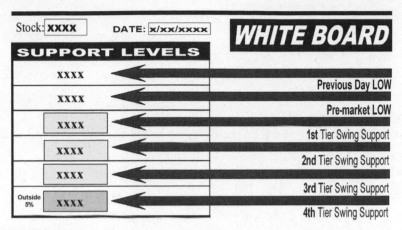

FIGURE 8.1 Sample Whiteboard Chart: Support Levels

Stock: **XXXX**   DATE: **x/xx/xxxx**   *WHITE BOARD*

RESISTANCE LEVELS

Outside 5% **XXXX**	4th Tier Swing Resistance
XXXX	3rd Tier Swing Resistance
XXXX	2nd Tier Swing Resistance
XXXX	1st Tier Swing Resistance
XXXX	Pre-market HIGH
XXXX	Previous Day HIGH

FIGURE 8.2 Sample Whiteboard Chart: Resistance Levels

stock. If it's a swing *long* you're seeking to fusion trade, then you'll only be trading *long* positions that day, and your whiteboard will only show *support* levels. And if it's a swing *short* you're seeking to fusion trade, then you'll only be trading *short* positions that day, and your whiteboard will only show *resistance* levels.

Also note that you may have to switch the pre-market price level with the previous-day price level, depending on which is lower/higher. And as I show in the third example here, the pre-market levels take out the first tier swing level, so now you're trading off pre-market levels.

■ Sample Fusion Trade #1

I'm starting with the simplest setup and then progressing to more involved and advanced fusion trading scenarios. All were taken directly from my online trading room. Figure 8.5 illustrates the normal process of gathering the intra-day levels in the early morning during pre-market, and then the opening bell decision regarding which levels to trade. I use IBM in this first example of a first-tier swing trade setup. Figure 8.3 shows the swing entry setup.

The first *indicator* I looked for was the *pre-market H/L price*. On March 23, 2015, pre-market was trading between 162.00 and 162.80. At that time I also had a *first-tier swing resistance price level* at 163.31. The current price was trading *within $3* of the *swing entry* of 164.31 ($1 past 163.31). This information was all I needed to decide to fusion trade that stock that day.

(To enable you to more easily grasp this, I've only listed the *resistance* levels, because the price went *up*. If the price had gone down, I could *not* have traded it *long*—not until it came *within $3 of the 149.42 first-tier swing price level*, which you can see in Figure 8.4, right column.)

Once the bell rang at 9:30, I had my pre-market *high,* which was 162.80. I also had my previous-day high of 163.00. In Figure 8.5

FIGURE 8.3 IBM One-Minute Chart

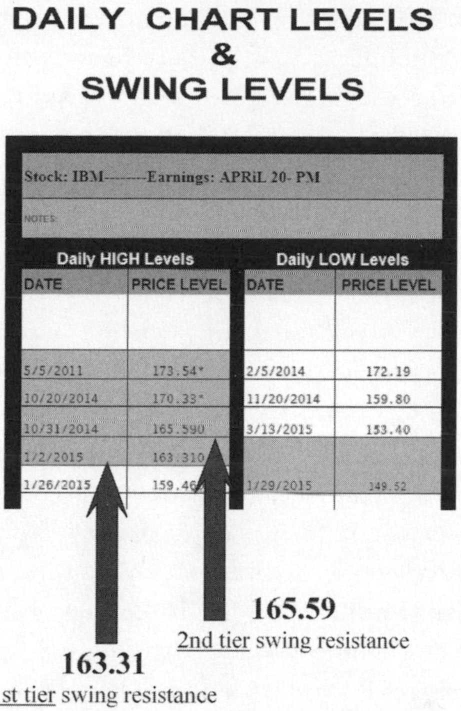

DAILY CHART LEVELS
&
SWING LEVELS

Stock: IBM--------Earnings: APRiL 20- PM			
NOTES:			
Daily HIGH Levels		**Daily LOW Levels**	
DATE	PRICE LEVEL	DATE	PRICE LEVEL
5/5/2011	173.54*	2/5/2014	172.19
10/20/2014	170.33*	11/20/2014	159.80
10/31/2014	165.590	3/13/2015	153.40
1/2/2015	163.310		
1/26/2015	159.46	1/29/2015	149.52

165.59
2nd tier swing resistance

163.31
1st tier swing resistance

FIGURE 8.4   Daily Chart Levels and Swing Levels

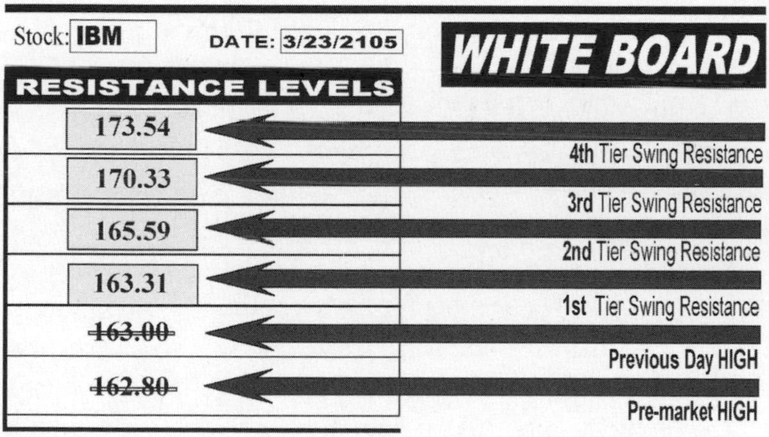

Stock: **IBM**   DATE: **3/23/2105**   **WHITE BOARD**

RESISTANCE LEVELS

173.54	←	4th Tier Swing Resistance
170.33	←	3rd Tier Swing Resistance
165.59	←	2nd Tier Swing Resistance
163.31	←	1st Tier Swing Resistance
~~163.00~~	←	Previous Day HIGH
~~162.80~~	←	Pre-market HIGH

FIGURE 8.5   Whiteboard Price Level on IBM (for 3/23/15 trading)

you'll notice that I had all my levels in numerical order. This particular setup was going to be fairly easy because I had no intra-day levels to trade leading into the first-tier swing entry (I knew all my intra-day levels and, as I've previously instructed you to do, I had them ready when the bell rang).

Accordingly, you can see that Figure 8.4 shows *only* the *daily* price levels, and it also shows which of the dailies were *swing* levels. You will be writing these levels on your own whiteboard each morning. Also, note in Figure 8.5 that I put a strikethrough line on both the pre-market and previous-day *high* price levels. Why? Remember the Golden Rule: *I cannot have two levels within 50 cents of each other.* So in this case I simply deleted those price levels from my whiteboard.

Now that I knew exactly what price level was next in line to trade, all I did was wait for it to hit. (The waiting is the hardest part.) I'd done all the homework and prepping. My price levels were correct and I had my plan. I just needed the *164.31 swing entry* price level to trigger. Once it did, I entered the trade (Figure 8.3).

"How many shares do you trade?" you might ask. Forget it. Don't even go there. Just worry about yourself and what your own capital buying power allows, and your own experience with this system. Remember: the hardest part of all day trading is knowing how many shares to buy/short at any given price level. In this one example, I've made things clear and simple: I'd been waiting for the entry price of 164.31 to hit. When it did I placed my *sell short* order.

When you're first learning this system, you'll only trade *100 shares* on each entry. In other words, in this example you would have *shorted 100 shares* at the 164.31 price level.

Also keep in mind that this is a *first-tier* entry. So realistically, as a beginner, you would be waiting for the second tier to hit before you'd enter. But the main lessons here are to know *where* your first-tier entry is, and *when* the trade cycles through. You need to keep track of when the price hits 164.31 and then *retraces back a full $2.00 to 162.31*. (Or it may profit $1.00+ at the close—recall the *50% profit rule*.) Either way, if the swing tier profits and you should have exited, this means the first tier is over. You would have profited $200 with a 100-share block trade, or $100+ with the 50 percent profit rule.

You might not have entered at all, and that's fine, but you still would have needed to recognize exactly when the trade ended. You must always be on top of your price levels, and also when the first tier is done, and when the second tier becomes the first tier. In other words, once the 164.31 swing level retraced for a profit, *the current second tier at 165.59 became the new first tier.*

Are you a little bit lost at this point? I understand. It will take more examples and real-world application before this makes any sense. During my training program, this is certainly one of the tough parts. And you're just reading, not driving—just looking at the map.

Let's finish this trade and move on. I entered short at 9:41 on March 23, 2015. That was when the price *initially* hit 164.31. I immediately threw a cover/buy order for my $2 profit at 162.31. I waited all day, the price never hit, so then I *held* my swing overnight. Such moves are perfectly normal, especially for this particular stock. Compared to my other, more volatile stocks, like TSLA and LNKD, IBM is a slow mover.

Now look at Figure 8.6, a five-minute map of a three-day period. The next day, the price never hit my target of a $2 profit at 162.31. So I held for another night. Finally, on March 25, 2015, the price dropped early in the morning. My exit price hit and I exited with my $2 profit. The first-tier swing level of 164.31 was now over, and the

FIGURE 8.6   IBM Five-Minute Chart

new first tier was 165.59 (the previous second tier). The reason why 165.59 became the new swing level is because it never hit it, thus making it the next level to trade when/if the price went back up.

■ Sample Fusion Trade #2

On March 27, 2015, I used TSLA, my most volatile stock. Depending on when you're reading this, you should be able to back-test the price levels used here on most charting platforms using the *daily chart*.

Because TSLA moves so fast, I always recommend that with that stock, you *do not try a fusion trade off the first tier*. That's especially true when the first tier is so close to the second tier—in this case it's exactly $3 off. A three-dollar gap may sound like a lot to you, but if you know TSLA, it's not much. For instance, note the huge gap between the second tier of 184.32 and the third tier of 177.22 in Figure 8.7.

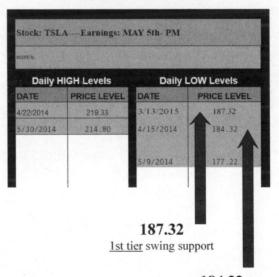

DAILY CHART LEVELS & SWING LEVELS

Stock: TSLA---Earnings: MAY 5th- PM

NOTES:

Daily HIGH Levels		Daily LOW Levels	
DATE	PRICE LEVEL	DATE	PRICE LEVEL
4/22/2014	219.33	3/13/2015	187.32
5/30/2014	214.80	4/15/2014	184.32
		5/9/2014	177.22

187.32
1st tier swing support

184.32
2nd tier swing suppor

FIGURE 8.7 Daily Chart Levels and Swing Levels—TSLA

This means the first tier was really risky for starting a fusion trade. This is where most of my trainees struggle, or they flat-out break this rule by fusion trading off a first tier, and find themselves in deep water.

Also note that on this particular day the first tier swing of 187.32 actually missed, meaning it came within 25 cents of entry, and then pulled back for $2. So the first tier could not have been traded anyway. I finally started fusion trading off the *second tier swing price level* of 184.32.

I resolved the situation by using *two* intra-day newly formed levels (new lows of the day) as my fusion entries leading into my *second tier* swing entry. This setup would become two separate trades, all in one day. The first trade would be a $400 profit and the second trade off the actual swing level would be the standard swing trading $200 profit ($2 pullback on 100 shares). The end total would be a $600 profit on this one fusion trade setup.

Again, you will always start with 100 shares on each entry, so bear in mind that $600 is the *minimum* that could have been made on this setup. Eventually, when you master this system and have enough capital, you can enter more and make more.

In Figure 8.7, note the price levels I had to work with at the opening bell on 3/27/2015. I had my current swing supports, the *second tier* being 184.32.

Figure 8.8 is my whiteboard. It shows my price levels organized in numerical descending order. Notice that I crossed off the pre-market support because it was more than $3 off my second tier swing entry of 183.32, and the previous day high of 189.70 couldn't be traded because the market opened *below* this price level at 189.11. If I wanted to fusion trade into my swing, I would need to wait for newly formed intraday lows that were within $3 of my swing *entry price*. I'm boxing that up big and clear:

> Your fusion entries must be within $3 of your swing entry price, *not* the swing level.

In this case my second-tier swing price level was 184.32. My swing entry was $1 past that level, so it was 183.32. Therefore I was looking for newly formed intra-day levels that were within $3 of

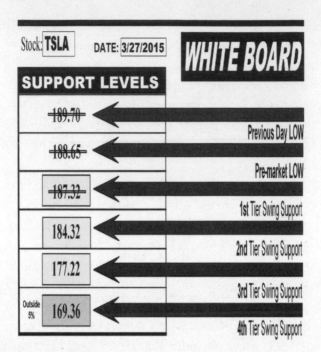

FIGURE 8.8 Whiteboard

183.32. This translates to *any newly formed* intra-day low price at or below 186.32.

On March 27, 2015, my first support formed within $3 of my swing entry price was the 185.70 intra-day low at 9:57 A.M., as indicated in Figure 8.9. So my first fusion entry would be 25 cents past that intra-day level. Once the price dropped to 185.45 at 10:17 A.M., I entered my first 100-share fusion trade.

At this point, you would have had two options. Once you entered at the 185.45 intra-day level, you could have simply recognized a 15-cent profit and then exited the trade. Then you could have waited on the sidelines until a new intra-day low formed and/or the actual swing entry hit. You know that when you're first learning this system, I want you to just take the 15 cents. But in this example I'm showing you what I do when I fusion trade, and what you will do in the future.

I waited for the full $2 profit on all entries (or I would close at 50% or more). In other words, after my first entry off the 185.45 price level I was hoping to exit at a $2 profit, so I needed 187.45 to hit,

TSLA 1-minute chart

1st intra-day support within
$3 of swing ENTRY
185.70

1st ENTRY off
intra-day support
185.45

EXIT on 200 share trade
186.80

EXIT on 100 share SWING trade
185.32

2nd intra-day support within
$3 of swing ENTRY
184.40

2nd ENTRY off
intra-day support
184.15

ENTRY off 2nd tier SWING level
183.32

FIGURE 8.9   TSLA One-Minute Chart

and—it didn't. So I went to plan B, which was to wait for a new low to trade and/or a swing entry to hit.

Not long after my first entry, a newly formed intra-day low was created at the 184.40 price level (the 10:17 candlestick in Figure 8.9). So I decided to make my second entry off this. Once it hit initially, I was going to enter at 184.15. This happened at 10:27.

Note that the entries are at least 50 cents apart (remember the Golden Rule). And in most cases I like my intra-day entries to be $1.00 apart, especially with a highly volatile stock like TSLA. This is a perfect example of how each stock needs to be traded slightly differently, according to its speed and volatility.

Now I had 200 shares off two intra-day levels. At that point my average price on my 200-share position was 184.80. I was looking for a *$2 pullback* on my current *fusion* 200-share setup, or I would enter my third trade off the swing at 183.32.

It turns out that the stock reversed for my $2 pullback on the first 200 shares, *before* it hit my swing. This is always a great trade! *As soon as it hit 186.80* at 11:00 A.M., I took my $400 profit. After that, the price began to drop again toward my original swing level—that was *still* in play. So I waited for the second tier swing to hit next.

It took all day for the second-tier swing entry of 183.32 to hit. At 2:39 P.M. I entered my swing trade at the 183.32 price. At this point I was still looking for a $2 profit on my 100-share position, which had now become a swing. I needed the price to reverse to 185.32 for a full $2 profit. The price actually reversed just before the bell rang, during my final-hour rally to get my full $2.

Now look closely at Figure 8.9, particularly the huge drop *after* I entered my swing trade at 183.32, the time being 2:39 P.M. By 3:09 P.M., the price had dropped all the way down to 181.41. So the price *dropped almost $200 in the red before it pulled back*. Not only was this normal, but keep in mind that the third tier was 177.22. In other words, the price could have dropped all the way to 177.22 before reversing.

Welcome to swing trading! You need a thick skin to ride these trades out. If you can't handle this rollercoaster, you'll never become a pro-trader. Believe in your levels and have confidence, and on every single trade be prepared to be dipping deep in the red *before* the trade reverses back into the green. It's all about knowing your swing levels, and choosing the correct levels to begin fusion trading. Some stocks you can fusion trade off the first tier, and with others you need to wait for the second or third tier. This takes weeks of training to master. So again, don't assume that you can fusion trade off a first tier on all stocks.

■ Sample Fusion Trade #3: An Advanced Fusion Trade

In this fusion trade example I use FDX. We'll focus on the swing support level first-tier of 168.03. The first day the price dropped within $3 of the first tier swing was on March 24, 2015, but it took until the next day to hit the entry level of 167.03.

On the right-column side of Figure 8.10 I show the *daily levels* that highlight the current swing support levels.

In this example the swing *entry price of 167.03* hit in pre-market trading. When this happens to you, you need to adjust your swing *entry* price to reflect the pre-market low price. Trying to trade off of pre-market for a swing entry is more advanced and requires more precaution, so I'll box it up for you:

> If your swing entry price hits in pre-market, you should wait for the *next* swing tier to hit. Or you trade off the pre-market H/L for your swing entry.

DAILY CHART LEVELS
&
SWING LEVELS

Stock: FDX---Earnings: MARCH 18th - AM			
NOTES:			

Daily HIGH Levels		Daily LOW Levels	
DATE	**PRICE LEVEL**	**DATE**	**PRICE LEVEL**
12/8/2014	183.51***	2/26/2015	173.42
1/22/2015	181.49	2/2/2015	168.03
2/18/2015	180.05	12/17/2015	163.57
3/17/2015	178.6	9/25/2014	157.04
11/11/2014	172.88	9/11/2014	150.01

168.03
1st tier swing support

FIGURE 8.10   Daily Levels

I chose to trade the pre-market low before waiting for the second tier swing level to hit. Note that the opening price on this day was much higher than the pre-market low. This happens from time to time, and it only means that the stock had a lot of volatility in pre-market trading. The reason why I couldn't trade the *previous day low* of 169.16 was because the first-tier swing of 168.03 had already broken in pre-market. So your first entry should be off pre-market low in this case, or you would wait until second-tier swing support hits.

In Figure 8.11, I crossed off the previous-day level of 169.16. I also crossed off the 168.03 first-tier swing level, but that does not mean the first tier swing had cycled through. It was still valid, but I had to adjust my entry to be off the pre-market low. This is a perfect example of how intra-day levels can dictate your swing price *entry*.

My *first swing entry* had to be *50 cents past* the pre-market low price of 166.95, making it 166.45. It *didn't pull back* on March 25, 2015,

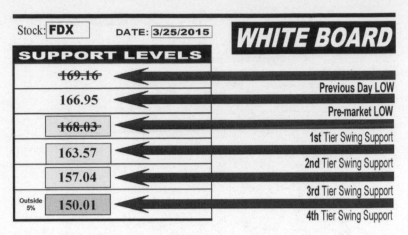

FIGURE 8.11 Whiteboard—FDX 3/25/15

for my $2 profit, nor did it close above 50 percent of my profit. So I *held* overnight. This was fine because it was a swing trade.

Do not confuse trading the pre-market intra-day level as an intra-day trade.

Remember, I was trading the first-tier swing, but it hit in pre-market, so I simply adjusted my swing entry price to reflect the pre-market low, which was 50 cents past. So again, my first-tier swing *entry* price was now 166.45, and not 167.03 ($1 past the first-tier swing of 168.03).

The next day I was looking for the price to pull back to 168.45 for my $2 profit. If that were to happen, then the first-tier swing would be done, but the price did not go up. Instead it dropped even more. Now I was looking to *fusion trade into the second tier support of 163.57*.

In Figure 8.12 I logged the 3/26/2015 whiteboard price levels.

The first factor I need to point out is that the stock price on March 26, 2015, *opened* at 164.28. So I immediately checked off my previous-day low of 165.35. My pre-market low was 164.20. Keep in mind that I was within $3 of my next swing *entry*, which was off the second-tier swing level of 163.57. Therefore I decided to fusion trade. I entered my second 100-share block trade 50 cents past the pre-market low of 164.20, making it 163.70. I now had *200 shares* with the *average* of 165.08. I needed 167.08 to hit for my $2.00 profit.

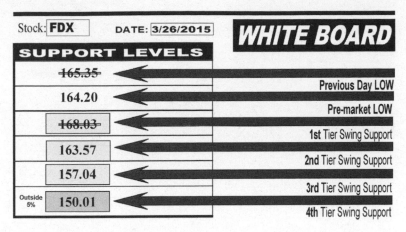

FIGURE 8.12   Whiteboard—FDX 3/26/15

Keep in mind that my second entry was a fusion trade off an *intra-day level* (pre-market low). I *could not hold* that level overnight. So I needed to sell 100 shares at the close, if I was in the green, or, if in the red, I would be forced to stop-loss on that 100-share intra-day portion of my swing trade. Either way, I was keeping my first 100-share swing entry of 166.45 until it profited $2.

On March 26, 2015, the price never hit the average of 167.08, but it did close at 165.49. That meant I could sell my intra-day fusion trade of 100 shares for a profit. I entered at 163.70, so at the close I recognized a $179 profit.

That was fusion trading at its best. I was able to make marginalized profits from an intra-day trade while in a swing position that had yet to make me money. In Chapter 9 of Part 5, I cover *pivot trading,* an advanced strategy. The fusion trade setup in Figure 8.13 is a prelude to what that's all about.

Now that I was out of the intra-day trade, I was still holding my original 100-share swing trade from the 166.45 level. The next day, on March 27, 2015, a Friday, the price went totally sideways. That meant no fusion trades and no exit. I would have to wait until Monday, March 30, 2015, to make any new decisions. For now this was a *hold* over the weekend.

Again, this is totally normal. You have a plan and you're in control of your strategy. You can go and enjoy your weekend; you will profit next week.

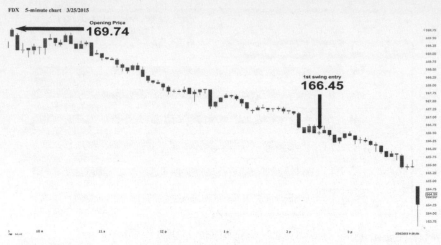

FDX   5-minute chart   3/25/2015

Opening Price
169.74

1st swing entry
166.45

FIGURE 8.13   March 25, 2015, Original Swing Entry

The charts in Figures 8.13 and 8.14 show the actual intra-day trade setups for this entire fusion swing trade on FDX. The trade lasted several days. I used five-minute candlestick charts so that it is easier to see the entire day of trading activity in each chart.

Figure 8.13 reflects the original swing entry that took place on March 25, 2015.

FDX   5-minute chart   3/26/2015

Exit 100 shares at close
165.49

Opening Price
164.28

Pre-Market Low
164.20

Fusion Trade (100 shares long)
163.70

FIGURE 8.14   March 26, 2015, Fusion Trade Setup

Figure 8.14 reflects the fusion trade setup that took place on March 26, 2015. This fusion trade happened within seconds after the bell rang.

Also notice in Figure 8.14 that the high of the day hit roughly one full dollar higher than the closing price where I exited. It's easy to look at the chart in hindsight and ask why I didn't sell when it was at the 166.50 price level. If you were to ask me that, I would respond by asking you: How did you know that was going to be the high? You could not have possibly predicted that. What I can indeed predict is my own steadfast consistency. For instance, I was waiting for my $2 profit as always. Again, I needed the price to hit 167.08, and it never hit. So I kept holding till the close. That was my plan to begin with. Either way I profited. The key lesson here is that you need to stick to your plan—stick to the system. This just happened to be a very low-volatile day so the price never hit my $2 profit target. All I am concerned with is not holding my intra-day fusion position overnight.

So my plan was twofold: simply hold intra-day for my $2 profit, or wait till 3:39 P.M. and close out my intra-day 100-share portion of the 200-share swing trade with either a small loss on the 100-share fusion trade or a small profit on the 100-share fusion trade. I happened to profit the $179 on this particular day. And I held the swing 100-share original position overnight.

In Part 5 on advanced trading techniques I will show you what to do if the 100-share fusion trade was in the red at the close. For now, just understand that you are still in a swing with the original 100 shares and can intra-day fusion trade while holding that position.

> *Note:* You need to make sure your current broker has your account set so that if you are trading the same stock with multiple 100-share entries/exits, the account is set to "cost basis," meaning the most recent exiting trade will always close out the potion that is in the green and not the red. This way you can recognize your intra-day fusion profits while holding your ordinal swing position for days. This is certainly an area covered in my training program.

Figure 8.15 reflects the non-activity trading session on March 27, 2015 (Friday). No trades were placed. I held the original swing trade position over the weekend (for you, that would be a 100-share

FDX   5-minute chart   3/27/2105

OPENING PRICE
165.05
(3/27/2015)

FIGURE 8.15   March 27, 2015, Non-Activity Trading Session

position). The price does drop a bit, but I was waiting for the second-tier 163.57 to break. The second-tier swing *entry* of 162.57 never hit on this day, so no trade. And, no fusion trade could be made because the low of the day broke well past 2 P.M., and I didn't want to risk the stock not retracing that late in the day—again, no trade.

Figure 8.16 reflects the non-activity day on March 30, 2015 (Monday). I held the original 100-share swing position over the

FDX   5-minute chart   3/30/2105

OPENING PRICE
165.05
(3/30/2015)

FIGURE 8.16   March 30, 2015, Non-Activity Day

weekend. The price starts to head up, in my direction, right after the bells rings. Recall, I needed 168.45 to hit so I could exit the swing trade. Also, there was no fusion intra-day trade simply because the price was heading up all day and never broke the low of the day at 164.98.

If the price had reversed *within the first two hours* of trading, then I would have fusion traded the intra-day low of the day. It didn't, so no fusion trade. I held swing position overnight again.

Tuesday (March 31, 2015) was another sideways day. There were no opportunities to fusion trade. So I held again overnight.

This would be a good time to remind you that I am certainly trading other stocks while in this holding pattern on FDX. I am gathering all my whiteboard levels each morning on my other 8 to 10 stocks that are in my online trading room.

You as a beginner may only be trading this FDX trade exclusively, but that doesn't mean you can't be watching and paper trading other stocks for the experience while waiting on your profits from this current (FDX) swing trade.

Keep in mind, if you get hyper-focused on your single position, you will most likely get emotional and restless. Do not allow your emotions to force you to stray from this system. Furthermore, there are fusion trades to be made in this FDX swing-hold, as I just showed you. So remain vigilant! Get your whiteboard price levels each morning.

This particular setup has been *five* trading sessions since we entered original first-tier swing on March 25, 2015. Again, this is totally normal. Sometimes a swing will pull back within minutes, and sometimes it runs to the fourth tier and takes all day; in this case it's been uncommonly sideways in the market, so FDX is also trading relatively sideways, and therefore our swing exit is not hitting right away.

At this point I will be looking to exit anything over 50 percent of my profit. Or I will exit by reentering another fusion trade that gives me $1.00 on a 200-share average fusion trade. Recall, I have already recognized $179 on this overall trade setup with my previous fusion trade. We will see what happens the next trading session on Wednesday (April 1, 2015), or later.

Note: I have been documenting this trade in real time — that's how confident I am in my own system. This will profit, but I cannot tell you exactly which day the swing will pull back for my profit.

Figure 8.17 reflects the setup that took place on April 2, 2015, when I exited the swing trade. This swing trade took six full trading sessions to conclude. I ended up taking $1 profit (50% of target).

Why? As mentioned previously, because this trade was taking so long. I typically will take 50 percent of profit target if holding a first-tier swing trade for more than three days. But you *must be aware* that the first tier *is not over*. Recall, the first-tier swing was 168.03. So the standard entry was 167.03 (not my fusion entry). Therefore, the price need to pull back to at least 168.03 for the first tier to have cycled through.

I was able to exit on April 1, 2015, because I fusion traded it. Here was my fusion trade (noted in chart 2.3). The pre-market low was 165.45 and my previous-day low was 164.99 (on 3/31/2015). I eliminated the pre-market because it was within 50 cents of my previous-day low. So I made my first fusion intra-day entry off the 164.99 previous-day low price levels. I *entered* my fusion trade with 100 shares, 50 cents past, so my entry price was 164.49. So my average price on my original 100-share swing position and the

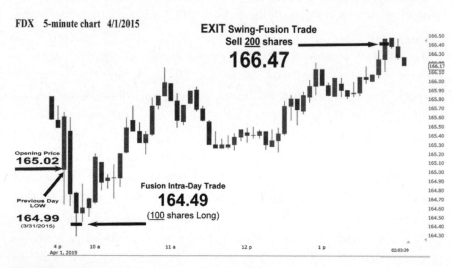

FIGURE 8.17   April 1, 2015, After Exiting Swing Trade

current 100-share fusion position is 200 shares at 165.47 ([166.45 + 164.49] / 2).

I was only looking for $1.00 profit. The price hits 166.47 at 1:49 P.M. on April 1, 2015. I exited the trade with a net $200 profit.

■ Final Words on Fusion Trading

You will most likely only enter your intra-day fusion setups during the first two hours of the market due to high volatility. Therefore, it would be wise to not try to fusion trade after 2 P.M. After 2 P.M. you should simply wait for *the actual swing entry to hit*. If your next swing level doesn't hit, then no trades should be made after 2 P.M.

This 2 P.M. advice is not a rule that applies across the board, and I certainly do not follow this advice myself. This rule is meant for beginners to the system, because you are not in rhythm with your new stock.

To recap, the fusion of a trade is essentially used in two scenarios: when your swing entry hits in pre-market and you have to adjust your new swing entry price, and/or when the current price is within $3 of your next swing entry price—you then begin intra-day trading using the Golden Rules.

In Part 5 you can expect to see more fusion trades. In addition I will be showing more advanced strategies such as *pivot trading* and *side line trading*. But first you need to completely understand how fusion trading works.

## PART V

ADVANCED RULES AND PROCEDURES

## CHAPTER 9

Maximizing Net Profits and Minimizing Losses on Overall Trade Setups

When it comes to explaining on paper, this chapter is by far the most difficult. Not being able to describe it in *real time* on interactive charts created a huge challenge for my editor, and is frustrating for me as a coach.

As I worked on this book I found myself doubtful about including the most advanced strategies. I thought that perhaps I should only reveal them one-on-one to those under my direct training, and not fling them out here capriciously. In the end I decided to add them, regardless of my misgivings. I figured some readers might desire the option to try advanced methods on their own. If they floundered and lost money or otherwise needed guidance, they would know where to find me.

But just as I've often mentioned—and it's even truer in this chapter—I'm afraid of what can happen if you try something tough with *real* capital and *no* formal training. At the risk of driving you nuts with my nagging, I'll reiterate that here you're only seeing the framework, the map of my Fusion Trading, and the map and the road are not the same. That's especially true when the unknown terrain gets denser and more convoluted and you're down in it all by yourself.

Advancement in any profession takes formal direction and coaching. It requires a guide who knows the terrain. As a seasoned director in day trading, I decided to *omit* the chart setups that would illustrate the strategies you'll find in this chapter. Why? Because I've learned that if I show one example on paper, novices lacking training will mimic that setup and apply it across the board in all situations and lose their shirts in the process.

Sorry; it's for your own good. My strategies, and especially my advanced strategies, can only be learned adequately by doing them repeatedly in my one-year training program. Sure, you can learn it all alone by trial and error. That's a choice you have every right to. But I'm not going to push you out of the helicopter over that dense terrain, not alone. You can do that jump on your own.

I do offer the framework of all complex tactics so you can see all their potential, and I do list the rules on procedures for each. That way you can start digesting the logic and have some clear rules to memorize.

> *Warning:* If you don't apply the rules properly, this system will *not* always work, and your *net profits* will be diminished.

The most perfect examples are specific situations where I instruct you to stop-loss—where I tell you to exit a trade in the red—because of my stringent risk management rules. In tandem I show you advanced rules and strategies that help you recapture those losses. You learn how to *gain back the losses you incur* in the very next trading session or within a few days. The point is to have your overall trade eventually become a net profit.

Overall refers to the fact that a swing trade isn't over just because you exited. Recall from Part 3 that your swing *stays in play* until the first tier and/or the average of all tiers hits its profit target, typically at $2. This means you can always reenter the trade, and at an even better price level, and ultimately gain back profits. Those new profits on the same swing trade can be allocated toward your previous loss. This means that your net result can eventually become a green trade.

I may have lost you at this point—my apologies. For now just remember this:

> Just because you had to take a loss, that doesn't mean the trade is over.

Once you've learned the following rules and you're applying them consistently, only then will you be closer to mastery of this system. Of course, on paper it sounds easy. I can assure you it's not. Think of the map as opposed to the jungle. You really have to work for your trade to become a *net profit*—especially if you had to stop-loss. I like to refer to this process as *wrestling* the trade. The advanced strategies in this chapter are the best tools I know, to date, that will help you *wrestle a losing trade back into the green*.

Now you may want to know: "How do I stop-loss but still gain a net profit on the entire trade setup?" The advanced rules you're going to read about are designed to save your butt in two ways. They'll prevent you from losing in one devastating swing trade by keeping you on the sidelines. They'll also help you recapture small losses, soon after you *strategy-exit*, by reentering at better price levels.

That's enough about losses. These advanced rules are not just to help you when you're in the red; in certain situations, they can help you increase your profits. For instance, when you're learning how to both trade from the sidelines and trade during earnings season, you'll gain knowledge of how to trade in 200-share block trades or higher, not limiting yourself to 100. Also, you'll allow profits to run for $4+ and not just $2 max.

Now I'll define the advanced strategies. They are:

- Pivot trading
- Sideline trading
- Trading earnings release

■ What Is Pivot Trading?

This is a term I came up with to describe the process of stop-loss when it's used at the market close. The trade can be either a straight swing or an intra-day fusion. The action of the pivot is to *wait* until the next day. The object of the pivot is to reenter that stock at a better price than when you closed yesterday.

When you reenter, you use the fusion-trade strategy. After that execution, you allow your profit on the new trade to run far enough to recapture the loss of the day before. That amount will usually exceed it. Typically you'll capture $2, just like with any swing trade and/or fusion trade. But I'm warning you, there's much more to this advanced strategy than what you're reading on paper. The most complicated factor, as I've told you before, is that all stocks must be treated slightly differently when applying these rules and procedures, and timing is everything.

For instance, when trading TSLA I may choose to pivot trade by reentering on a third tier. But when trading GS I'll reenter the trade after the second tier. Or maybe I'll choose to fusion trade an intra-day level *past* the first tier.

Those are all options that can only be determined by the specific stock that you're trading. Here on paper I offer a dangerously oversimplified framework to pivot trading, just to minimize your confusion.

This strategy can only be used in certain situations.

For instance, if the trade is *not* in a current (first-tier or higher) swing, there *can't* be a pivot trade. In other words, you must have at least entered the original trade after a swing level has hit. This is one reason why I always tell beginners to wait for the second-tier swing to hit, prior to their first entry. Why? Because they don't yet know how to pivot trade, and neither do you. So beware!

Once you've mastered this system, you should use pivot trading in *three* primary situations:

1. You enter off a first-tier swing, but you *don't hold* it overnight, because you really should have been waiting for a second-tier swing to hit. So you stop-loss on your first-tier swing entry at the 4 P.M. close. Next day, you pivot to recapture your small loss by reentering off either the same price you closed at or the second tier—and you choose *whichever is higher*.

2. You've been fusion trading and your intra-day entries didn't profit, so you stop-loss at the 4 P.M. close with however many shares were being traded off the intra-day levels. The next day you reenter with the same amount of shares as with the fusion intra-day trade at the stop-loss, but *not until you wait for the swing tier entry*. In other words, on the next day you don't try to fusion trade the exact same levels again.

3. You stop-loss your swing positions on the day of an *earnings release*. You reenter the trade the next day, or if the release is in pre-market, later in the day.

The *Basic* Strategy for Entering Pivot Trades

Luckily the pivot trade process is exactly the same as my swing and fusion trade strategies. The only difference is that you're trying to get back the losses of the previous day. So your *exit price* can be tricky, not to mention the loss may have made you too emotional, causing you to make more mistakes.

Remember these general pivot trading rules:

- You can only reenter if the trade is *still in play*.

- You can only reenter if your reentry price is *higher than your stop-loss price the previous day*.

- In order to get your reentry, *you follow the fusion trading rules*.

Those rules imply that if you can't reenter, that means your stop-loss is *final*. Remember that when your trade's still in play that means your swing levels *haven't yet cycled through* for the profit. The profit is either $2, or the 50 percent rule. You absolutely have to know where your swing levels are—always. If not, your pivot trading will be a disaster, and that's something I can promise.

If your trade is over, *no longer in play*, and you're in the red on your *overall* trade—move on. You can't win them all! It happens to everyone. I certainly log stop-loss trades throughout the year, meaning the *overall trades were net loses*. But they're mostly small losses and they don't happen often.

"Why not?" you may anxiously ask. I rarely lose on an overall trade because I failed to recapture the next-day profits on the same trade still in play. The same can be true for you. If you get to be good at wrestling your trade back to green after a stop-loss, you won't lose overall, either. The thing to remember is that *most of your trades won't require a stop-loss*.

Net profits are the main motive, but as a novice it's much more important for you to follow the rules and procedures and maintain a vigilant focus. Make that your motive for now and the profits will certainly follow.

I look over this chapter that has additional rules to the ton of rules you've already looked at, and I want to ask: Are you lost yet? At this point, my trainees always are, even on one-on-one phone conferences with my undivided attention. Even when I'm showing them chart setups in real time, focusing on one guy at a time, they still need several trade setups to get it. I warned you. Advanced strategy is extremely involved. But note that it's based on clearly defined rules and procedures already set down in this book. There's no guesswork with this system.

Pivot trading isn't easy. It gets pretty ugly and scary. It's not for the faint of heart. But if you've been doing everything right, you'll seldom need to resort to it.

■ Sideline Trading

Sideline trading is pretty much what the wording suggests. You're off the beaten path, and you're hovering. You're waiting to enter a trade when it's past the standard initial entry point(s), and you enter at optimum levels *if/and/or when* they trigger. And *for every sideline entry, you follow the fusion rules*. You can't dive back in simply because the price is higher or lower than the first tier.

A great example of sidelining is when a trade is in play and I'm waiting for the *first-tier* entry price to trigger, and when it does I don't enter—I wait. I wait for the price to move even further in my favor. I wait for the *second-tier* swing level to trigger—that's my *initial* entry.

That is a classic sideline trade. But you'll recall that it's also a safety measure. In Part 3, as I introduce you to swing trading, I direct you to sideline. I warn that trading a first tier is very risky for beginners, and that you should wait for the price to run further before you enter the trade.

So it seems that you, the beginner, will be using a very advanced tactic as you learn how to trade. It seems like a pretty big irony. But not so fast—nothing's advanced, not if you enter the first trade with only 100 shares. Yes, I do tell you to enter a trade at a second tier or higher, but safety first: 100 shares, period.

Right now I'm introducing you to a *higher* sideline kind of trading, which means 100+. Once you've mastered this system, you can start with 200 shares on the first entry, or 300, or even 500—whatever your capital permits.

Think about it this way. If I were to enter a first-tier swing trade with 100 shares, and then the price ran against me, my trade would have triggered more swing entries. So let's say I reentered off the second tier with another 100, the third tier with another 100, and finally a fourth tier with 100. That translates to a 400-share position with an average price. With sideline trading I could have simply waited for the fourth tier to hit and entered the swing trade with 400 shares. This is a perfect scenario, especially when you consider that *I had no average price*. Instead I entered at the optimum fourth-tier price level. That sounds great but it only works if the fourth tier hits.

This strategy of course has its downside. The obvious benefit is you're much better positioned to enter the trade initially, and profit sooner than you would in a first-tier entry. But you can miss the trade altogether. If the price reverses for a profit just after the hit of a first-tier swing level, then your sideline trade is over. Most swing trades reverse before they hit the second- and third-tier entries. So, yes, you may be safe on the sidelines, but no cigar!

Here are some sideline rules:

- When you enter a sideline trade, you must follow the standard swing and/or fusion rules.

- You can't enter if the trade is no longer a swing trade (not in play).

- You can't reenter at the same level twice in one day.

- You can't add more shares to your position simply because you enter at a higher or lower tier.

- You must always have enough capital remaining to reenter again after your initial sideline trade.

Here's a scenario I like very much. I've missed the huge move at the opening bell, so the stock is currently trading off a fourth tier. Right out of the gates, the stock price jumps $8+. When this happens, I can come in and sideline-trade the stock, so long as the fourth tier is still a fourth, in other words, *still in play*.

Here is the caveat: How many shares do I initialize the trade with—100, 200, or 400? For yourself, you know the answer: safety first. You, the beginner, must enter with only 100 shares. Entering at the fourth tier does *not* guarantee that the price will *not* run another 5 percent against it—it can. I'm a pro, so I know how to make those decisions and not lose my shirt. You, however, are a babe in the woods, so you stick with 100 shares or less. You can sideline trade with 25 or 50 shares.

Here's the good news. If you do capture a fourth tier, you can run the price back for a $4 profit, and sometimes even much more. Of course this requires much more knowhow than what's learned from reading this map. But I can tell you this. If you know your current swing profit exit, then that is your exit point; it's as simple as that. For instance, suppose your fourth-tier entry (*long* position) is at 210.00, but the average of the first, second, third, and fourth tier is 215.00. That means the swing trade profit target price is 217.00 ($2 profit). Therefore you can *technically* run the price back to 217.00, which means you earn a juicy $7 profit ($700) on the trade.

I assure you that it's not that easy. But my example above does give you a feel for how sideline trading works. It also sheds light on why my online swing trading room shows profits as "minimum." The swing room shows trades that all start with the first tier. But in reality many of them were entered at higher or lower levels (sideline trades) and with more than 100 shares per entry, thus producing much larger profits. You will read about this in Chapter 10, my trading room chapter. For now, bear in mind that sideline trading certainly offers more options.

■ Earnings Release Trading

I assume that most of you already know what an earnings release is. So I'm not going to waste paper or your time to explain it. But I will remind you that earnings release dates are the times when you need to be on high alert and ready to apply additional rules and procedures, or else stay away and do nothing at all.

Four times a year—that's every three months—earnings results are announced by each publicly traded company. So every three months I have to switch gears and rev up the engines. That translates to getting up earlier with larger cups of coffee and quadruple-checking all my whiteboard price levels, and much more.

Typically there's an average of eight stocks in my trading room at any given time. That means I experience on average about *32 earnings release periods each year*. And so will you when in my one-year program. I've been doing this a long time and I can tell you that those are hands-down the most complicated periods to trade in.

In my first book I flat-out tell you to *not trade the day before or the day of an earnings release*. If you don't have a system to weather this storm in, you should hightail it for shelter. These periods are chaotic and utterly unpredictable. As a novice, you should just take a break.

Regardless, I've developed a plan—a methodical system of trading on those treacherous earnings release dates. I certainly do not run for shelter—my novice days are far behind me and there are huge profits to be made!

Here I address the *basic* rules and procedures for trading on those dates. Earnings postings get released in *pre-market* hours (5 A.M. to 9:29 A.M. EST) or *aftermarket* hours (4 P.M. to 8 P.M. EST). Previously I've mentioned that the pre-market session is *8 A.M. to 9:29 A.M.*; this is partially true. Most high or low prices do hit during that hour and a half. On earnings release dates, however, you need to see the *entire session* from 5 A.M. to 9:29 A.M. Keep in mind that most brokers allow for you to place trades during both periods, especially direct-access brokers. But just because you *can* trade then does not mean that you *should*.

For earnings release I have two ironclad *Golden Rules*. Remember them just like the others:

---

1. Never hold a position into an earnings release.
2. Do not enter a positon *during* the release of the earnings.

I could stop my advising right here. If you follow those two invaluable rules, your trading results will drastically improve. But I have much more free advice I want to share.

The following rules-based procedures will save you from losing mountains of hard-earned cash and dealing with nights of cold sweats and 3 A.M. to 4 A.M. shivers. If you use the rules properly, you can make double or triple your normal amount of profits during earnings season. I do!

Procedure #1

If the earnings release date is *within five trading sessions, never enter a swing position.* Trade other stocks instead and wait until after earnings to enter and/or reenter the trade. You can still fusion trade right up to the release, but only if you've mastered this system. However, no matter how experienced you are, you *never hold* swing positions overnight, not that close to the date.

"Why not?" you may want to know. Because you're risking huge overnight gaps that typically start to develop as the big day approaches. Besides, if you're holding a swing position, this Golden Rule applies: you need to be prepared to stop-loss, or exit with a partial profit, just before the earning results are released.

For instance, if earnings are released in *aftermarket*, then you need to exit the trade at 4 P.M. *on that day*. If the earnings release is the next morning in pre-market, then you exit at the close *the day before*.

But there are always situations where this five-trading-session rule has some wiggle room, and it can happen in either direction (but wiggling is not to be done without coaching). For instance, with some stocks in some situations it's okay to enter a swing trade only three trading sessions out, and with other stocks you may want to not enter a swing within 10 trading sessions of the date.

"Why?" you might ask. It's about *which swing tier is hitting* and *which stock* you're involved with, and of course your *skill level* figures in. But this is where my written instructions get useless. At this point I need live interactive charts to explain this any further.

Just be aware that you shouldn't enter a swing position, and you should never hold overnight, when approaching the earnings release dates. And make sure you're aware of the dates at all times—*put them all on your whiteboard.*

The easiest way to find these dates is on Yahoo Economic Reports. Go there and search "earnings release dates." Then be prepared for the dates to change. You need to periodically check for that, especially when you're within five trading sessions. Luckily, if the date does change, it's almost always pushed out to the next day or else to a few days later.

Procedure #2

When the day comes you simply wait on the sidelines and log two simple price levels. All you need is the *highest and lowest prices* that hit in this intensely volatile and high-volume trading period. I think you know what I'm talking about. Within seconds of a release hitting the wire, most of our stocks fluctuate up to $20 or more, and do so in either direction. I take 100 percent of the guesswork out of this crazy period. I suffer no guessing at all—just the *waiting.*

You *wait* for the turbulent trading to end— I mean you're down for the counting. You batten down the hatches and stay there. Pre-market or aftermarket, no matter: each will reach a *very definable* high and low price. Recall my intra-day trading rules on gathering pre-market levels in Part 2. It's just like that. You log the high and low that took place in that turmoil. Then once again you *wait* for the next trading session to begin.

The hard part is learning what the heck those price levels mean, and what to do when the market reopens. If you haven't considered those highs and lows, then you're trading totally blind when the next trading session opens. It's the same as the reason for knowing the importance of pre-market data every morning, when you trade on a normal day.

Procedure #3

Be aware that the earnings release high/low price is *good for only the next trading session. It's only good for one day.*

The daily chart does *not* register aftermarket and pre-market price levels, not in each candlestick. Please don't ask me why. I'm still trying to figure that out. It has something to do with Wall Street not wanting the average investor or trader to know what price levels are being traded before and after the bell rings. My system taps into whatever they don't want us to know. But that's a conspiracy theory, and I don't have time for all that. Even if it's true, I don't care. What matters is my system works. It will only stop working if trading aftermarket and pre-market is discontinued by the SEC, and that will never happen.

So let's get back to the basics. It's critical that you write down the high and low prices after earnings release—or at least be aware of them. Have them on your charts the day of. If the release happened in aftermarket, then you have all night and the next early morning to make your order entry decisions and having all that time is great. Luckily, most releases are then.

If the release is in pre-market, then you may want to sit it out. Even trainees in my program typically bow out of pre-market releases. Why? Because right up until the bell rings, you don't know the true high/low, and you only have seconds to make your decision, and that takes a lot of experience.

Let's assume you have earnings release levels that formed in aftermarket trading. Take those levels and compare them to your swing levels, and then ask yourself these two questions:

1. Which swing *resistance* tier(s) did the *high* price of aftermarket break?
2. Which swing support tier(s) did the low price of aftermarket break?

Once you know the swing tiers that did or didn't break, then you know what price you *can* enter the initial trade at, or what price you *cannot*.

As I'm writing all this I'm shaking my head, but I'm not finding this funny. I'm aware that complex factors arise when I make my decision to enter a trade based on an earnings release—factors that will trip you up.

To help paint a picture of how I trade during an earnings release, here is a mock trade setup. I'm using BIDU. I like BIDU because it always releases earnings aftermarket. And chances are when you read this it will still be priced between $100 and $250, so you can use it for your own back-testing on the next release that comes up.

Let's assume the release has just occurred. It's 4 P.M. and I'm watching the price fluctuations. I don't really have to sit here and do that; I'm just letting it be visual music. The only thing I have to do is log the high/low, after the close of aftermarket.

It gets to be 8 P.M. EST, and now I have my results. The high price was $230 and the low price was $205. The first thing I look for is what general direction the price moved in. Did it go up or drop? In this case the price shot up and hit the $230 high. So now I'm glued to my swing levels, particularly the *highs* (the resistance levels), and I'm pretty sure the 205 low won't be my focus, come morning.

Here are my swing (resistance) levels *prior* to the earnings release:

207.25
211.40 tier 1
214.65 tier 2
222.50 tier 3
228.30 outside 5%
238.50 outside 5%

In this scenario my *first-tier* swing resistance is 211.40. Good thing I didn't enter at that price prior to earnings release, because the earnings release high of $230 took out all three tiers and also the 228.30 swing level.

So what price do I enter at? Hold on—this is where it's critical to *stop*. I need to wait and see what happens in pre-market the next morning, when it could go higher than $230. When 5 A.M. EST comes around, pre-market opens at 225.50. So the price dropped a bit overnight. By 9:30 A.M., I have my high of pre-market logged. It's 226.75. Now what level do I enter at? Do I trade the pre-market high of 226.75 or do I wait for the 230.00 to hit?

Which one of those would you do? Always go with the higher. But what about the 238.50? That will be today's *second tier*. If it hits, I will trade off the 230.00. But I'm not done here. I also have to wait for the price to go past the 230.00 *by $2.00* (not $1.00). My first entry, or *short* position, will be at $232. As usual, this all begs the question: Did I lose you?

After utilizing all these rules and procedures, I finally came up with one single entry price that I'm *waiting* to see hit. If it doesn't hit, I have no entry. It's that simple. If it does hit, I will be entering the trade at an extremely overbought price level. This is why I'll ride it back down *$4, not $2*. And I'll enter *200 shares or more*.

That was just one example of hundreds I could demonstrate. And if we were looking at real charts, I could show you several past trades based on earnings. Here I just need you to see how important the earnings release price levels will be, and how they impact your current swing levels.

Before my trainees completely understand them, pivot trading, sideline trading, and earnings release trading require at least 50 trade setups while I'm coaching them in our one-on-one scheduled phone conferences. Again, you have to be deeply in rhythm with your individual stock, and skilled in this fusion trading system, to make these advanced tactics work or even to grasp their potential.

## PART VI

TRADING AND TRAINING WITH DAY TRADER JOSH

## CHAPTER 10

My Trading Room and How It Works

I would like to start by reminding you that if I enter at a certain price level with a certain amount of shares, that doesn't mean you should be entering at that level or with that many shares. At this point I don't have to tell you why, but for the sake of risk management I'm telling you just the same, because being a nag about your not going broke is three-fifths of who I am.

189

As a beginner in this system, you haven't mastered it yet, and you may have less capital than I do. So you shouldn't be trading a first-tier swing level and you should only be trading in 100-share blocks. In most other online trading rooms that offer you instruction, that's not how it is. What you'll find there is counterintuitive and risky to the point of insane. Most are bogus, or they don't provide correct information. The operator/trader is offering only what works for him, with no clue what works for you. Many online trading rooms make their calls *after* the fact, meaning they reverse-engineer what happened in-market that day, and then they don't post their trading results until after the closing bell. Of course, this makes them look really profitable. Does the word *illegal* come to mind here? Many online trading rooms are thinly disguised scams. At the very least they offer their trade setups not caring that their entry/exit levels may not be the right ones for *you*.

With that said, are you ready for some good news? My online trading room bridges that quagmire and makes this ride *relatively* safe for you. I say relatively because with all trading activity there are inherent risks—the biggest risk being that you are your own worst enemy.

Contrary to what most other trainers have been doing, when I first designed my trading room, I aimed for transparency. From its beginnings and right to the present, my system has reflected exactly what the trading room does. The best way to do this is to show my swing levels *prior* to the day they will hit—in many cases I know the level weeks ahead of it hitting. This way there is no denying that my system works. For instance, in this chapter you'll see images of my "Future Setups" portion of the swing room. Here is where I show all the stocks I'm trading and the next swing level to hit on each stock. Once those swing levels hit, I document each trade setup.

When the price levels have dates and exact support /resistance levels to trade, *prior* to the price hitting, there's no way this system can be altered. This eliminates your confusion or suspicion of something bogus. I'm there to make consistent profits and show you how to do it. I have absolutely no incentive to hype up a worthless system.

My online trading room is the key to my training program. Why? Because I found the price levels with my methodology. Therefore my trading room is your training wheels while you're working on mastery. In this chapter I include several screenshots of it. You will notice that there are two parts. I have my *daily chart room* (Figures 10.1 and 10.2) and the *swing trading room* (Figures 10.3–10.6).

Day Trader Josh's

DAILY CHART LEVELS

TRADING DATA FOR BOTH INTRA-DAY & SWING

UPDATED LAST ON: 4/13/2015   QUICK NOTE: earnings this thursday on GS

FIGURE 10.1   Day Trader Josh's Daily Chart Levels

Stock: BIDU----Earnings: APRIL 22- PM

NOTES:

Daily HIGH Levels

DATE	PRICE LEVEL
11/13/2014	251.99
11/26/2014	248.74
12/26/2015	237.43
1/23/2015	234.67
1/9/2015	232.99

Daily LOW Levels

DATE	PRICE LEVEL
11/20/2014	236.1
11/6/2014	233

Stock: AAPL----Earnings: APRIL 21- PM

NOTES: main focus will be on SHORTS off all-time highs...no LONGS

Daily HIGH Levels

DATE	PRICE LEVEL
all-time high	133.6
3/9/2015	129.57
11/25/20142/4	120.51
12/29/2014	114.77

Daily LOW Levels

DATE	PRICE LEVEL
2/26/2015	126.61
3/12/2015	121.63
12/1/2014	111.27
01/16/15	104.63

FIGURE 10.2 Daily Chart Room

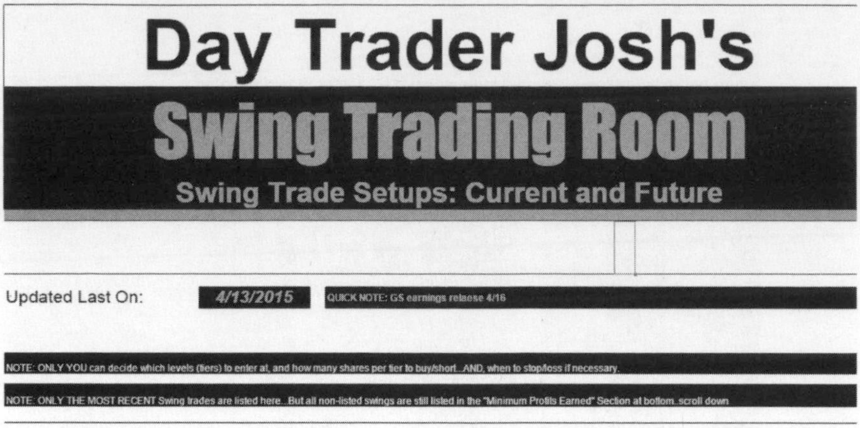

Day Trader Josh's
Swing Trading Room
Swing Trade Setups: Current and Future

Updated Last On: **4/13/2015** QUICK NOTE: GS earnings release 4/16

NOTE: ONLY YOU can decide which levels (tiers) to enter at, and how many shares per tier to buy/short...AND, when to stoploss if necessary.

NOTE: ONLY THE MOST RECENT Swing trades are listed here...But all non-listed swings are still listed in the "Minimum Profits Earned" Section at bottom..scroll down

FIGURE 10.3   Day Trader Josh's Swing Trading Room

The daily chart room is only specific to the daily levels for each stock (Figure 10.2). As you know by now, this room is the key to the entire system. Recall how important the *daily levels* are and how critical it is to constantly update them. My daily levels room does exactly that for each and every stock I trade.

The swing-trading room is more involved. It includes:

- Most recent trades that have been completed (Figure 10.4)

- The future trade setups and stocks most likely to hit levels today (Figure 10.5)

- The minimum profits to date (Figure 10.6)

Figure 10.6 shows the minimum profits that could have been earned with my system—minimum because when you examine the chart, you'll notice that each tier is 100 shares. This means that if you're trading with more than 100 shares, then more profits can be made. Also, the chart *doesn't include all the intra-day fusion trades* that were made during the wait for a swing to hit.

Fusion trades, *for a master trader*, can constitute as much profits as the normal swing trades produce. I just don't list them because there are far too many, and I simply do not have the time to document every single intra-day trade (fusion trades). If you choose to enter my training program, then this trading room will be your focus, and this will be in sync with my one-on-one coaching conference calls. You'll have access to it for a full year.

CURRENT - Swing Trades

STOCK: GS

1st ENTRY	
Date	3/10/2015
Time	9:50:00
# of shares	100(LONG)
Price	184.59
Daily Level	185.50
PreMarket H/L	skip 1st tier

2nd ENTRY	
Date	
Time	
# of shares	
Price	
Daily Level	
PreMarket H/L within 5% of tot	

3rd ENTRY	
Date	
Time	
# of shares	
Price	
Daily Level	
PreMarket H/L within 5% of tot	

EXIT	
Date	3/12/2015
Time	9:30:00
# of shares	100
Average Price	184.59
Profit/loss	**$200.00**

4th ENTRY	
Date	
Time	
# of shares	
Price	
Daily Level	
PreMarket H/L within 5% of tot	

5th ENTRY	
Date	
Time	
# of shares	
Price	
Daily Level	
PreMarket H/L within 5% of tot	

ENTRY NOTES: 1st tier hit in PreM, so 2nd tier was first entry

EXIT NOTES: two day hold...almost closed above 50% both days.. but didn't..so full $2 profit

---

CURRENT - Swing Trades

STOCK: LNKD

1st ENTRY	
Date	2/6/2015
Time	10:12:00
# of shares	100(short)
Price	299
Daily Level	297
PreMarket H/L	

2nd ENTRY	
Date	
Time	
# of shares	
Price	
Daily Level	
PreMarket H/L within 5% of tot	

3rd ENTRY	
Date	
Time	
# of shares	
Price	
Daily Level	
PreMarket H/L within 5% of tot	

EXIT	
Date	
Time	2:53:00
# of shares	100
Average Price	299
Profit/loss	**$400.00**

4th ENTRY	
Date	
Time	
# of shares	
Price	
Daily Level	
PreMarket H/L within 5% of tot	

5th ENTRY	
Date	
Time	
# of shares	
Price	
Daily Level	
PreMarket H/L within 5% of tot	

ENTRY NOTES: PreMarket was 297, so $2 past rule for earnings trade, double profit $4 (295)

EXIT NOTES: pulled back like clock work for $4 profit

FIGURE 10.4 Swing Trading Room—Most Recent Trades

FUTURE SETUPS
Swing Trade Setups (3-Phases)

Levels Held (10-Days or more)	
TSLA (LONG)	177.22
TSLA (SHORT)	214.80 (1st)
AAPL (LONG)	121.63
AAPL (SHORT)	129.57
GS (LONG)	earnings on 16th..be careful!
GS (SHORT)	earnings on 16th..be careful!
IBM (LONG)	153.4
IBM (SHORT)	165.59
LNKD (LONG)	215.52
LNKD (SHORT)	276.18**
ILMA (LONG)	N/A
ILMA (SHORT)	197.37
BIDU (LONG)	202.2
BIDU (SHORT)	220.83 (1st now)
FDX (LONG)	163.57 (1st now)
FDX (SHORT)	178.6 (1st now)
BA (LONG)	N/A
BA (SHORT)	158.91

Levels in process of forming (LESS THAN 10-Days)	
TSLA (LONG)	
TSLA (SHORT)	
AAPL (LONG)	
AAPL (SHORT)	YOU MUST STAY ON TOP OF LEVELS
GS (LONG)	LESS THAN 10-DAYS ...possible swings
GS (SHORT)	
IBM (LONG)	
IBM (SHORT)	
LNKD (LONG)	The key to mastering swing trading is
LNKD (SHORT)	knowing your newly forming DAILY levels,
ILMN (LONG)	and...
ILMN (SHORT)	Knowing when a 1st tier swing is current & ended
BIDU (LONG)	
BIDU (SHORT)	
FDX (SHORT)	
FDX (LONG)	
FDX (SHORT)	

Levels CAN hit TODAY (WITHIN $3 of 1st tier)	
BIDU (SHORT)	220.83 (1st)
BA (SHORT)	154.91 (1st)
TSLA (SHORT)	214.80 (1st)
FDX (SHORT)	178.46 (1st)
IBM (SHORT)	165.55 (1st)

FIGURE 10.5 Future Trade Setups

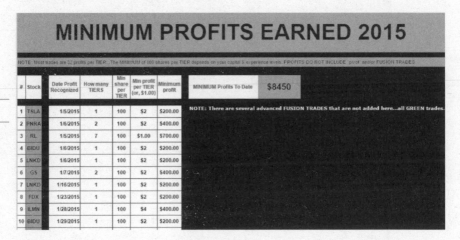

MINIMUM PROFITS EARNED 2015

NOTE: Most trades are $2 profits per TIER...The MINIMUM of 100 shares per TIER depends on your capital & experience levels. PROFITS DO NOT INCLUDE 'pivot' and/or FUSION TRADES

#	Stock	Date Profit Recognized	How many TIERS	Min share per TIER	Min profit per TIER (or, $1.00)	Minimum profit	MINIMUM Profits To Date	$8450
1	TSLA	1/5/2015	1	100	$2	$200.00	NOTE: There are several advanced FUSION TRADES that are not added here...all GREEN trades.	
2	PNRA	1/6/2015	2	100	$2	$400.00		
3	RL	1/5/2015	7	100	$1.00	$700.00		
4	BIDU	1/6/2015	1	100	$2	$200.00		
5	LNKD	1/6/2015	1	100	$2	$200.00		
6	GS	1/7/2015	2	100	$2	$400.00		
7	LNKD	1/16/2015	1	100	$2	$200.00		
8	FDX	1/23/2015	1	100	$2	$200.00		
9	ILMN	1/28/2015	1	100	$4	$400.00		
10	BIDU	1/29/2015	1	100	$2	$200.00		

FIGURE 10.6 Minimum Profits to Date

## CHAPTER 11

The Day Trader Josh Training Program

So many times I've been asked: "How do you trade full-time and also find the time to coach?" The simple answer is that I don't do both at once, not during the first two hours of the market. The deeper way to answer the question occurs to me in two versions, one short and one long. The short answer is I enjoy teaching others. I love to show others how to make consistent profits.

Day trading stocks independently tends to be a solitary profession, and I'm not a loner. I enjoy interacting with my trainees, and also my graduates who become professional traders. I love being there when my trainees first realize this system actually works. That pleases me more than anything that I may achieve by myself.

The long-story reason is that, someday, I plan to have my own private equity trading floor on or near Wall Street, or sunny San Diego, preferably both. In order to have highly seasoned traders on my floor, I need to sufficiently train them. I need to develop and thoroughly groom our future trading group. I'm currently in the process of a double evolution. I'm building my trainee/graduate base, and most importantly, I'm acquiring the skill set required in a master private equity day trading coach.

It's extremely important for you to know that my coaching is one-on-one. All live-trading trainees and graduates have access to the same online trading room, but our phone conferences are entirely one-on-one, always just you and me speaking. That way I can set the right pace—right for your schedule and your own progression in practicing and learning the material. You have one full year to master the system, so there's no rush to learn if you've got a "real" job or any other fulltime commitment.

The length of my mentorship program blows away the standard industry teachings. Most prominent training programs show you how to set up your accounts with *only* a pay-per-trade online brokerage, and they show you a few standard trading techniques. Then, after they've gouged out your wallet to the tune of thousands of dollars, they throw you to the wolves.

The training industry tuition range is 3K–7K. If they charged a lot less money, it wouldn't be so bad. Think about it: you pay for only three to five days of instruction, and your fee comes to more than most state university registration fees for an entire four-month semester.

On the contrary, my *initial core training* takes a *minimum* of six weeks. This core training happens throughout the one-year program. This is because you must practice the Day Trader Josh system during market hours, particularly the first two hours from 9:30 to 11:30 A.M. EST. You're not required to trade every day, and you can do the six weeks spread out and broken up—consecutive isn't important. The goal is to thoroughly grasp the system whenever you can be there.

Similar training programs charge the same fee or higher, but they only last a few days. You can't learn the mechanics and skill set of day trading in just a few measly days, and you can't really do it in a classroom setting, which is what you'll find in most corporate training programs. One-on-one is essential.

■ Program Details

As you've already seen in Chapters 1 through 5, you will learn *both* intra-day and swing trading. When combined, that's my Fusion

Trading system. You will start off learning intra-day trading and all the pertinent rules and procedures, and then you'll advance to swing trading, a system that requires more experience and skill. You will learn how to Fusion Trade by using both intra-day and swing trading setups. Finally, you will learn the advanced strategies, including pivot trading, sideline trading, and trading during an earnings release.

My *intra-day strategy* is based on making 15-cent profits ($15) at specific pivot points. You will only be trading *one* stock while you learn intra-day trading, and all of your trades will be limited to that one stock in the program. Typically, when you're trading one stock, you'll place between one and five roundtrip trades in the first two hours of the market. After you master that phase, you'll eventually start adding more stocks. More stocks means more trades.

Depending on your rate of progression, the intra-day trading phase of the course takes up the first two or three weeks. It's important to not rush yourself. Learning the system thoroughly is all that matters here. The final three or four weeks are for learning swing trading and Fusion Trading. The more advanced strategies will be learned over the remaining year of the program. The key to my system is knowledge of both strategies and using both to maximize profits. For instance, you could go three days straight with no swing entry. You would use that time to focus completely on Fusion trades.

When you progress to learning my *swing-trading strategy*, your trades will run for $1.50–$2.00 profits ($150–$200). Depending on your capital, you will have the option of trading more than 100 shares. As you learn to carefully maneuver, the greater risks you begin to take will lead to greater rewards.

■ Learning Objectives

- Learn *why* you must know intra-day setups *before* you place swing trades.

- Learn *why* you place orders directly from the Level 2 quote chart in *real time*.

- Learn *why* you trade in 100-share blocks.

- Learn *why* you intra-day trade stocks priced $100–$250.

- Learn *why* you take consistent profits per trade of $15 (intra-day) and $200 (swing) per 100-share trade.

- Learn the mechanics of *fastkey* order execution (critical for intra-day trading).

- Learn how to place over 20 roundtrip trades in the first two hours of the market (intra-day and swing trades combined).

- Learn how to trade with *pay-per-share* brokers at 40 cents per 100-share trade.

- Learn chart analysis using one-minute candlesticks and using the *daily* candlestick chart (*real* price-level strategy).

- Learn how to recognize newly forming intra-day support/resistance and *previous* support/resistance.

- Learn how to place real-time limit orders—getting in and out of trades in seconds.

- Learn how to *tier* into a trade (as opposed to averaging in): this is an advanced alternative to relying on a *static* stop-loss.

- Learn how to use the Day Trader Josh trading room for *both* intra-day and swing.

- Learn how to use the *Lightspeed* demo trading platform—this will blow you away!

- Learn how to back-test your intra-day and swing trades: homework is essential.

- Learn what *tiers* are best to enter at for *swing* trades.

- Learn how to turn an intra-day trade into a swing trade.

- Learn over a hundred rules and procedures that make the system work consistently.

- Learn how to Fusion Trade.

■ What the Price Includes

- Learning the Day Trader Josh entire trading methodology and graduating to pro-trader status within the one-year period.

- Eight or more one-hour phone conferences (one-on-one training and strategy sessions with me for the *initial core training*).

- After core training, continuous 5-to-15-minute phone conferences and emails for an entire year.

  - Virtual in-person mentorship: back-testing your trades (one-on-one phone conferences).

  - Experiencing Day Trader Josh trading in real time (one-on-one phone conferences).

  - Training on a fastkey order execution *demo* trading platform.

- After core training, my personal help with your *live* trade setups that you perform on your own.

  - *Free* access during the one-year program to my Day Trader Josh Trading Room.

  - My personal guidance through the four very risky and tricky *earnings seasons* during the one-year program.

  - After you've learned the entire system, *each month* the option of asking me questions on *two* specific trade setups.

■ Recap

You can learn my Fusion Trading system all within six weeks, or spread the sessions over a longer period. Regardless, you'll be under my wing for an entire year. You'll have access to my trading rooms for one full year.

Contact me for scheduling start-dates.

ABOUT THE COMPANION WEBSITE

This book has a companion website, which can be found at www.wiley.com/go/daytrading. Enter the password: dipietro123

The companion website offers an opportunity to view and download full color versions of all the figures from the book.

As you've seen, in this book there are over a hundred rules and procedures. With that said, virtually every trade setup can go horribly wrong if you neglect even one of the rules or don't follow proper procedures. This is not only true for you. This is true for all Wall Street day traders and for traders at all private equity firms all around the world.

In the professional world of day trading, you don't just lose capital when you make a big mistake. You get fired. You take the proverbial walk of shame off the trading floor. In the interest of not losing your money, you need to approach my Fusion Trading system with exactly the same caution and prevention that the pros use to keep their jobs.

I can't tell you how many times I've been contacted by graduates who tell me the horror stories about their bad trades. They all have one thing in common. They all admit that they knowingly made a mistake.

As a trainer my main objective is to coach you to the point where you can back-test your trades at any time and know exactly where you should have entered and exited, or whether you should have entered at all. After learning my system beside me, one-on-one, you should have the ability to make, on your own, the proper decisions in real time while trading.

For instance, if you know that the swing trade you just placed was not actually a swing level (meaning the daily level never held for 10 days), then you should also know you jumped in too soon. You should know you made a mistake, especially if you held this position overnight. As a graduate, did you really need me to tell you to stop-loss? I certainly would have if you were still under my wing.

I'm concluding this book with a quick reference to several of the most important rules and procedures that can be understood here on paper. The rest can only be taught in real time while you're being coached by yours truly.

The following must be hardwired into your trading psychology and memory. Let's begin with what we always begin with: intra-day trading.

I will not list the Golden Rules again, but I will stress that if you break any one of them, your intra-day trades will be drastically off. For instance: the most detrimental mistake a trader can make is to start intra-day trading when *more than $3 off their swing level*.

I'll use TSLA as an example. TSLA can easily run $10+ in one single trading session. If it does skyrocket that far in one day, chances are it's because it's either hitting or approaching a swing level.

I can show you in words here, no need for a chart. Suppose you trade pre-market high and you enter a short position 50 cents past the resistance level. So far that sounds like my system. But, without this given information, suppose you enter the short position at $200, and the first tier swing price level is at $210. You are now $10 off your swing level. So what should you have done? You should have used the Golden Rule to wait for the price to come within $3 of a swing level.

If you ignore the Golden Rule, you may just get lucky and your trade goes green, and you exit. Okay, but if you continue to break this rule, I can promise that eventually you will get burned. In most cases, the price will run the full $10 against your short position and hit the swing level. In this hellish scenario you will likely be very upset and worried. Meanwhile, I and my disciplined trainees and graduates will all be perfectly content. Why? Because *before* we started intra-day trading the short position, we all chose to wait for the price to come within $3 of the swing level. We all chose the correct process. We started looking for the newly formed intra-day highs that were above $207 (within $3 of the $210 swing level).

So you see, because you threw one single rule out the window, your trade went terribly wrong, your trade went deep in the red, while the rest of us trading the same system were profiting that very day, or we never entered to begin with and are safe on the sidelines.

Here's a list of factors that contribute to disastrous intra-day trades:

- You didn't wait for intra-day levels to come within $3 of a swing level.

- You failed to find the correct daily levels and know where your first-tier swing level was.

- You traded a first-tier swing level when you thought it was a second-tier swing level.

- You didn't gather the correct previous-day high/low price.

- You didn't gather the correct pre-market high/low price (recall, sometimes pre-market *starts at 6 A.M.*)

- You weren't aware of the earnings release date of your stock.

- You entered more than one intra-day position within 50 cents of each other.

- You tried to get more than a 15-cent profit when you hadn't mastered the fusion system.

- You didn't have whiteboard price levels ready and organized when the bell rang.

- You didn't stick with 100 shares max per tier/intra-day price level until you mastered the system.

- You *held* an intra-day position overnight.

Now we'll move on to swing trading.

First, you must *always* remember that all swing levels are daily levels, but not all daily levels are swing levels. The *10-day hold rule* is the key to knowing your swing levels.

Here's a list of factors that contribute to disastrous swing trades:

- You're not watching, or you lack the skills to properly watch, the daily chart every morning and night—you're not back-testing.

- You're not realizing that your swing level hit in pre-market trading session.

- You enter a swing trade within five trading sessions of an earnings release.

- You're trying to get more than $1.50–$2.00 on each swing tier.

- You are exiting your swing positions too soon and not recognizing your full $1–$2 profits.

- You're not realizing the speed and volatility of the new stock you add.

- You're not sticking with 100 shares max per tier/swing price level until you master the system.

- You *hold* a swing position overnight and into an earnings release.

Finally, let's cover fusion trading.

By now you know just how involved a fusion trade setup is. After you fully grasp the intra-day setups and are capable of determining your swing levels, only then will you have the skill set to tackle a fusion trade.

Here is a list of factors that contribute to disastrous fusion trades:

- You forget that, just as intra-day trading requires, a fusion trade can only be attempted when your intra-day price level comes within $3 of your swing.

- You don't make sure to close out your intra-day positions prior to 4 P.M., market close.

- You should be profiting only 15 cents of fusion trades, not the full $2, until you are formally trained.

- You are trying to fusion trade more than one stock per trading session, before you master the system.

Here's what you have to look forward to.

You will ponder whether you've learned enough from this book to try my fusion trading on your own, or whether you should go with my coaching. Before you decide what to do, and no matter which direction you take, please remember that this system takes weeks if not months of training prior to going live with real money. Even if you're in my training program, with the one-on-one advantage of my coaching, you will need at least six weeks of instruction before you're ready to trade live, and then another year before you master this system.

But once you master this system, you can certainly anticipate the upside of trading with more than 100 shares per tier. You can take $2 profits on fusion trades. With that said, the sky is the limit when you're properly tuned, with all four cylinders syncing, and you're not missing a beat.

Welcome to day trading stocks the Wall Street way!

AAPL (Apple Inc.), 47, 116
Aftermarket:
  avoiding trading in, 15, 17, 183
  earnings releases, 21, 94–95,
    181–182
  previous day high/low, 58–59,
    184–185
Amateur traders:
  breaks and, 4, 10–11, 25
  gambling mentality of, 23
  impatience of, 8, 9
Amazon.com, Inc. (AMZN), 47,
  97–100, 116
Apple Inc. (AAPL), 47, 116
Average daily volume, 34–35
Averaging down, 4, 14, 31–32
  avoiding reckless use of, 31–32
  nature of, 31
  tier-trading *versus,* 31–32

Back-testing, 102–106
  end-of-day intra-day trading
    activity, 105–106
  information needed for,
    102–104

real-time (current) intra-day
    trading activity, 104–105
  in swing trading, 119–120
Baidu.com, Inc. (BIDU), 46, 114,
    134–136, 185–186
Bankruptcy risk, 37
Bid/ask spread:
  average daily volume and, 35
  as critical for intra-day stocks,
    47–48
  ideal level of, 35
  on pre-market Level 2 charts,
    47–48
Black-box (high-frequency) trading
    systems, 35, 62
Body, of candlestick charts, 55, 56
Bollinger bands, 54, 60
Breaking news, 5, 21, 37, 50, 95
Breaks, 10–11. *See also* Sideline
    trading
  activities during, 11
  in controlling fear factor, 4
  due to news and economic
    reports, 28

Breaks, (*Continued*)
  importance of, 4, 10–11, 25
  in maintaining consistency, 27
  in maintaining focus, 5
Budgeting:
  during breaks, 11
  for every trade, 32
  importance of, 11, 18–19
Buying power:
  defined, 12
  of intra-day traders, 12–13, 14,
    19, 39
  in risk management, 12–14, 18,
    121
  of swing traders, 13, 14,
    121–122, 125, 130,
    133–134
Buy/long limit orders, 146

Candlestick charts:
  in back-testing, 102–106
  body, 55, 56
  daily, 62–64, 104, 110
  five-candlestick rule, 74–77, 89,
    110
  one-minute, 54–56, 87–88,
    91–92, 102–106, 152, 159
  sustainable support/resistance
    levels, 70–76
  wick, 55, 56
Capital:
  defined, 12
  equity calls/margin calls, 19, 39,
    121
  in intra-day trading, 12–13, 14,
    19, 39
  in swing trading, 13, 14,
    121–122, 125, 130,
    133–134
Capital/margin ratio, 12–14, 18,
    121

Close. *See* Aftermarket; Market
    close; Overnight positions
CNBC Business News Channel, 30
Coaching. *See* Training/coaching
Coffee, in maintaining focus, 5
Commissions:
  pay-per-share, 16, 38–42, 86
  pay-per-trade, 16, 38–42
  for swing trading, 16
  typical pro-trader trading
    volume, 40
Confidence. *See also* Fear factor
  demo (paper) trading for, 6, 7
  importance of, 6
  overconfidence *versus*, 6–7
Consistency, 26–27
  of average daily volume, 34–35
  breaks in maintaining, 27
  in controlling greed factor, 4
  highly regimented trading system
    for, 26–27
  of liquidity, 34–35
  overconfidence and, 7
  of price in stocks traded, 26,
    33–34, 45–48
  of profit levels in intra-day
    trading, 27, 48–50, 86–88,
    91–92
  of profit levels in swing trading,
    48–50, 117–118, 122–123,
    126, 129
  in stock-selection criterion
    system, 26, 33–34, 45–48
  of trade sizes, 27
  of trading, 35
Countertrend trading
    methodology, 7, 9, 22, 35,
    48–50. *See also* Fusion
    trading; Intra-day trading;
    Swing trading
  comfort with being in the red,
    147–148

countertrend reversal in, 53–54
retracing in, 48–49, 154
stop-loss orders in, 51–52, 94
CRM (Salesforce.com, Inc.), 125,
   127–130

Daily high, 59–60. *See also* Daily
   price levels in intra-day
   trading; Daily price levels in
   swing trading
in daily chart, 63
in swing trading, 110
on whiteboard logs, 68–74
Daily low, 59–60. *See also* Daily
   price levels in intra-day
   trading; Daily price levels in
   swing trading
in daily chart, 62–63
in swing trading, 110
on whiteboard logs, 68–74
Daily price levels in intra-day
   trading, 62–77
logging and organizing, 67–74
minimum of one daily price level
   within $3 of first entry,
   80–81, 84, 94, 152,
   157–158
prior price levels and, 57–60,
   68–74
rules for determining, 62–67
whiteboard logs, 68–74
Daily price levels in swing trading,
   109–113
avoiding trading every swing
   tier, 128–136
determining first-tier swing
   level, 112–113, 115, 118,
   132, 144, 152–154
resistance, 110–111, 118,
   124–126
rules for determining, 110–113
10-day hold rule, 111–112, 124

Day trading. *See* Intra-day trading
Demo (paper) trading:
during breaks, 11
in confidence-building, 6, 7
in controlling impatience, 9
in fusion trading, 149
Lightspeed demo, 105–106
in placing orders, 97–100
Direct market access (DMA)
   providers:
FASTKEY order execution, 41,
   96–106, 199
pay-per-share commission
   structure, 16, 41–42

Earnings releases. *See also* Earnings
   release trading; News and
   economic reports
avoiding holding positions into,
   21, 94–95, 181
avoiding trading on, 16, 181
history and consistency, 46–47
overnight gap of more than $10,
   66–67
stop-loss orders day of release,
   50
Yahoo Finance in monitoring, 29
Earnings release trading, 181–186
day of earnings release, 183–184
earnings release date within five
   trading sessions, 182–183
general trading rules, 181–182
nature of, 181
trading session following
   earnings release, 184–186
training/coaching for, 186
Economic news. *See* Earnings
   releases; News and
   economic reports
Emotional attachment, 34
Entry/exit strategy in fusion
   trading, 144–148, 152–169

Entry/exit strategy in intra-day
    trading, 88–95
  connection with swing setups,
    120, 140, 142–144 (*see also*
    Fusion trading; Swing
    trading)
  in controlling fear factor, 4
  market price barriers, 49–50,
    89–90
  overconfidence and, 6
  predetermined, 20–22
  rule of entry, 90–91
  rule of exit, 90, 91–92
Entry/exit strategy in pivot
    trading, 177–178
Entry/exit strategy in swing
    trading, 115–122,
    124–136, 152–169
  connection with intra-day
    setups, 120, 140, 142–144
    (*see also* Fusion trading;
    Intra-day trading)
  50 percent rule for taking
    profits, 117–118,
    129, 168
  rule of entry, 115–116,
    118–120
  rule of exit, 116–118
Equity calls/margin calls, 19, 39,
    121
Exercise, in maintaining focus, 5
Exit strategy. *See entries beginning
    with* "Entry/exit strategy"

FASTKEY order execution, 41,
    96–106, 199
  back-testing trades, 102–106
  keyboard keys, 96–97
  Level 2 streaming quote charts,
    97–100
  real-time trades (manual limit
    orders), 100–102

Fear factor:
  breaks and, 10
  confidence and, 6–7
  nature of, 3–4
  tips for controlling, 3–4, 10, 51,
    93–94, 147–148
FedEx Corporation (FDX),
    160–169
Fibonacci lines, 54
First-tier swing price level:
  5 percent rule in swing trading,
    113–117, 122, 124,
    126–127, 129
  in fusion trading, 152
  in swing trading, 112–113, 115,
    118, 132, 144, 152–154
5 percent rule in swing trading,
    113–117, 122, 124,
    126–127, 129
Five-candlestick rule, 74–77, 89,
    110
Focus:
  importance of, 4
  tips for maintaining, 4–5
FreeStockCharts.com, 102–105
Fusion trading, 137–169
  common mistakes, 204
  daily high/low, 59
  deciding trading options,
    148–149
  entry/exit strategy, 144–148,
    152–169
  importance of training/coaching,
    196–197, 201–205
  merging intra-day trades with
    swing trades, 109, 110
  minimum of one daily price level
    within $3 of first entry,
    80–81, 84
  non-activity trading session,
    165–167
  as term, 139–140

timing of trades, 169
Trader Josh Training Program,
      196–197
trading pre-market intra-day
      level *versus* intra-day trade,
      162–169

Gambling:
   day trading *versus,* 13, 23–25, 88
   nature of, 13
   reckless averaging down as,
      31–32
Gap rule, for daily level, 66–67
General market price barriers,
      49–50, 89–90
General Motors (GM), 30
Golden Rules, 78–95
   in confidence-building, 7
   in controlling greed factor, 4
   entry/exit strategy, 88–95
   entry price 25 or 50 cents past
      support/resistance level, 84,
      159
   initial entry off intra-day
      high/low or prior level, 83
   know second entry before
      entering first trade, 79–80
   maximum of three tiers for each
      trade setup, 81–82, 84–86
   minimum of one daily price level
      within $3 of first entry,
      80–81, 84, 94
   no two entries within 50 cents of
      each other, 83–84
   summary, 79, 145
   swing trading, 144–148
Goldman Sachs Group Inc. (GS),
      47, 114–115, 119, 176
Government regulation, 36–37
Greed factor:
   being on alert for, 49
   breaks and, 10

consistent profits and, 27,
      48–50, 86–88, 91–92
   day trading *versus* gambling, 13,
      23–25, 88
   impatience and, 8–9
   nature of, 3–4
   tips for controlling, 3–4, 10,
      78–79, 86–88
GS (Goldman Sachs Group Inc.),
      47, 114–115, 119, 176

High/low pre-market levels,
      57–58
Hours of trading, 19, 77, 169

IBM, 46, 48, 49–50, 130–134,
      152–156
Impatience, 8–9
   of amateur traders, 8, 9
   intra-day trading, 8–9
   swing trading, 107
   tips for controlling, 9
Intra-day trading, 43–106. *See also*
      Fusion trading; Swing
      trading
   approach to trading, 40
   back-testing, 102–106
   basic procedure, 26–27, 45–52,
      54
   breaks and, 4, 5, 10–11, 25, 27
   capital/buying power, 12–13,
      14, 19, 39
   common mistakes, 203
   consistency in (*see* Consistency)
   consistent profits, 27, 48–50,
      86–88, 91–92
   daily price levels, 62–77
   deciding trading options,
      148–149
   entry/exit setups, 88–95
   FASTKEY order execution, 41,
      96–106

Intra-day trading, (*Continued*)
  gambling *versus,* 13, 23–25, 88
  Golden Rules (*see* Golden Rules)
  impatience in, 8–9
  learning before trying swing
    trading, 107, 140–142
  minimum SEC capital
    requirements, 12–13, 14,
    19, 39
  price action in one-minute
    candlesticks, 54–56, 87–88,
    91–92, 102–106
  price levels in predicting
    reversals, 60–62
  prior price level
    support/resistance levels,
    56–60
  screen hardware
    recommendation, 54,
    104–105
  stock price, 33–34, 35–36,
    45–48
  stock-selection criterion system,
    7, 9, 33–37, 45–48
  strategy stop-loss, 20–22,
    50–52, 92–95, 174–175
  sustainable support/resistance
    levels, 70–76
  swing trading *versus,* 139–142
  three-tier setups, 81–82,
    84–86, 112
  Trader Josh Training Program,
    196–197
  25-cent market barriers, 49–50,
    89–90

Lag, 62
Leading indicators, 54, 60, 62
Level 2 quote charts:
  bid/ask spread in pre-market
    data, 47–48
  direct-access orders, 97–100

100-share block trades, 40–41
Leverage:
  avoiding holding margin
    positions overnight, 13, 17,
    24, 32, 121
  buying power as, 12
  capital/margin ratio, 12–14, 18,
    121
  equity calls/margin calls, 19, 39,
    121
  intra-day capital requirements,
    12–13, 14, 19, 39
  swing trading stop-loss orders,
    21
Lightspeed demo, 105–106
Limit orders:
  buy/long, 146
  for consistent profits, 27, 48–50
  in FASTKEY order execution,
    100–102
  predetermining price, 24
  standard, 101
LinkedIn Corp. (LNKD), 29,
    60–62, 64–65, 69, 70, 71,
    81, 143–147, 155
Liquidity, average daily volume
    and, 34–35

MACD stock charts, 54, 60
Margin positions:
  avoiding holding overnight, 13,
    17, 24, 32, 121
  margin calls/equity calls, 19, 39,
    121
Market close. *See also* Aftermarket;
    Overnight positions
  hours of trading, 19, 77, 169
  pivot trading, 21, 94, 163,
    175–178
Market makers (MMs):
  average daily volume and, 34–35

in FASTKEY order execution,
98–100
Market open. *See also* Pre-market
data
hours of trading, 19, 77, 169
news at open, 30
preparation for trading, 70–74
(*see also* Whiteboard logs)
Market price barriers, 49–50,
89–90
Market risk, 15–17
causes of overexposure to, 15
normal exposure to, 15
overexposure to, 15–17
tips for avoiding overexposure
to, 16–17
Market trading hours, 19, 77, 169
MSNBC, 21
Multi-tier swing trades, 127–130,
134

Newly forming price levels, 71–73
News and economic reports. *See
also* Earnings releases
avoiding trading on, 16, 181
breaking news, 5, 21, 37, 50, 95
breaks related to, 28
impact on entry/exit strategies,
21
at start of day, 30
tips for monitoring, 29–30, 37
types and impact on markets,
21–22
100-share-block trades:
advantages of, 40–41
for beginning traders, 13–14,
24, 27, 40–41
in controlling fear and greed,
3–4
for maintaining consistency, 27
pay-per-share commission
structure for, 16

to prevent overexposure to
market risk, 16
stock price in intra-day stock
selection system, 33–34,
35–36, 45–48
three-tier max strategy, 81–82,
84–86, 112

One-minute candlestick charts,
54–56, 87–88, 91–92,
102–106, 152, 159
Online brokers:
FASTKEY order execution, 41,
96–106, 199
pay-per-share *versus*
pay-per-trade commissions,
16, 38–42, 86
potential scams, 38–39, 78, 189,
196
Opening bell. *See* Market
open
Overconfidence, 6–7
dangers of, 6
indicators of, 6–7
Overexposure to market risk,
15–17
causes of, 15
normal exposure *versus,* 15
tips for avoiding, 16–17
Overnight positions:
gap rule for daily level, 66–67
intra-day, 32, 94
margin, 13, 17, 24, 32, 121
swing trading, 109–110,
117–118, 140–141

Pattern day trading:
buying power, 121–122
defined, 39
pattern identification during
breaks, 11
pay-per-share trading, 39

Pay-per-share commission
    structure, 16, 38–42
  features and benefits of, 38–42
  finding brokers, 40
  for pattern day traders, 39
  static profit level, 86
Pay-per-trade commission
    structure, 16, 38–42
  potential problems, 38–39
  for swing trading, 42
Personal/family issues, 5
Pivot trading, 21, 94, 163,
    175–178
  entry/exit strategy, 177–178
  general trading rules, 177–178
  nature of, 175–176
  situations for, 176–177
  training/coaching for, 178, 186
Pre-market data:
  avoiding trading in pre-market,
    17
  fusion trading, 150, 151,
    162–169
  high/low pre-market levels,
    57–58, 68–74, 120
  as key factor in stock selection,
    48
  Level 2 chart bid/ask spread,
    47–48
  prior price levels in, 56–60
  rhythm factor in stock price,
    141–142
  swing level entry price hits
    during, 120, 135–136
  trading pre-market intra-day
    level versus intra-day trade,
    162–169
Previous day high/low, 58–59,
    68–74
Prior price levels, 56–60

daily high/low
    (resistance/support),
    59–60, 68–74
  fusion trading, 150
  pre-market high/low, 57–58,
    68–74, 120
  previous day high/low, 58–59,
    68–74
  resistance levels, 56–60
  support levels, 56–60
  swing trading, 144
  on whiteboard logs, 68–74
Profit:
  consistency in intra-day trading,
    27, 48–50, 86–88, 91–92
  consistency in swing trading,
    117–118, 122–123, 126,
    129
  50 percent rule for taking
    profits, 117–118, 129, 168

Real-time trades (manual limit
    orders):
  back-testing, 104–105
  in FASTKEY order execution,
    100–102
Resistance levels, 56–60
  in avoiding reckless averaging
    down, 32
  in back-testing, 104–106
  confirming sustainable intra-day,
    70–76
  daily high, 59–60
  defined, 57
  entry strategy, 90–91
  first-tier swing price level,
    112–113, 115, 118, 132,
    144, 152–154
  pre-market high, 57–58
  previous day high, 58–59
  in swing trading, 110–111, 118,
    124–126

in tier-trading, 31
Retracing, 48–49, 154
Reversals:
  countertrend, 53–54
  price levels in predicting, 60–62
Rhythm factor, 46–47, 141–142
Risk management, 12–25
  budgeting in, 11, 18–19
  buying power *versus* capital in,
    12–14, 18, 121
  day trading *versus* gambling, 13,
    23–25, 88
  market risk in, 15–17
  nature of, 12–13
  stop-loss orders in, 20–22,
    50–52, 92–95, 174–175

Salesforce.com, Inc. (CRM), 125,
  127–130
Screen hardware recommendation,
  54, 105–106
Second-tier swing price level, 157,
  159–160
Selection of stocks. *See*
  Stock-selection criterion
  system
Short swing trading, 129,
  131–132, 150–151, 154,
  155
Sideline trading, 10, 178–181
  general trading rules, 179–180
  nature of, 178–179
  situations for, 180–181
  training/coaching for, 186
Start-up capital. *See* Capital
Stock price. *See also* Prior price
  levels
  consistency of stocks traded, 26,
    33–34, 45–48
  in intra-day stock-selection
    criterion system, 33–34,
    35–36, 45–48

one-minute candlesticks, 54–56,
  87–88, 91–92, 102–106,
  152, 159
  in predicting price reversals,
    60–62
  price action in one-minute
    candlesticks, 54–56
  resistance levels (*see* Resistance
    levels)
  rhythm factor in, 46–47,
    141–142
  support levels (*see* Support levels)
Stock-selection criterion system,
  7, 9, 33–37
  average daily volume, 34–35
  average intra-day price swings,
    35–36
  bankruptcy risk, 37
  consistency, 26, 33–34, 45–48
  current news, 37
  government regulation, 36–37
  importance of, 33–34
  key factors in, 33–34
  stock price range, 33–34,
    35–36, 45–48
Stop-loss orders, 20–22
  as automatic, 20
  to fix mistakes, 22, 50–51, 95
  in intra-day trading, 20–22,
    50–52, 92–95, 174–175
  pivot trading, 178
  predetermining price, 24
  strategy for using, 20–22,
    50–52, 92–95
Strategy stop-loss, 20–22, 50–52,
  92–95, 174–175
Stretching, in maintaining focus, 5
Support levels, 56–60
  in avoiding reckless averaging
    down, 32
  in back-testing, 104–106

Support levels, (*Continued*)
  confirming sustainable intra-day,
    70–76
  daily low, 59–60
  defined, 57
  entry strategy, 90–91
  pre-market low, 57–58
  previous day low, 58–59
  in swing trading, 110–111,
    143–146, 160–161
  in tier-trading, 31
Swing pivots, 80–81
Swing trading, 107–136. *See also*
    Fusion trading; Intra-day
    trading
  avoiding holding margin
    overnight, 13
  avoiding holding positions into
    earnings releases, 21,
    94–95, 181
  back-testing in, 119–120
  capital/buying power, 13, 14,
    121–122, 125, 130,
    133–134
  commission structure, 16
  common mistakes, 203–204
  consistency in, 26–27
  consistent profits, 48–50,
    117–118, 122–123, 126,
    129
  daily high/low, 60
  daily price levels, 109–113
  deciding trading options,
    148–149
  entry/exit strategy, 115–122,
    124–136, 152–169
  first-tier swing level, 112–113,
    115, 118, 132, 144,
    152–154
  5 percent rule, 113–117, 122,
    124, 126–127, 129
  Golden Rules, 144–148

  intra-day trading *versus*, 139–142
  learning intra-day trading before
    trying, 107, 140–142
  minimum of one daily price level
    within $3 of first entry,
    80–81, 84, 94, 152,
    157–158
  minimum SEC capital
    requirements, 121–122
  100-share-block trades in, 13–14
  overnight positions, 109–110,
    117–118, 140–141
  pay-per-trade commission
    structure for, 42
  resistance levels, 110–111, 118,
    124–126
  second-tier swing price level,
    157, 159–160
  short sales, 129, 131–132,
    150–151, 154, 155
  standard limit orders in, 101
  stop-loss orders in, 21, 50–52
  support levels, 110–111,
    143–146, 160–161
  swing pivots, 80–81
  10-day hold rule, 111–112, 124
  Trader Josh Training Program,
    196–197
  trading experience, 121–122,
    125
10-day hold rule, 111–112, 124

Tesla Motors Corp. (TSLA), 21,
    30, 47, 114, 156–160, 176,
    202–203
Tier-trading. *See also* Resistance
    levels; Support levels
  averaging down *versus,* 31–32
  determining first-tier swing
    level, 112–113, 115, 118,
    132, 144, 152–154
  Golden Rules, 78–88

multi-tier swing trades,
127–130, 134
nature of, 31
red-zone tier in swing trading,
126–127
three-tier max strategy with
100-share block trade,
81–82, 84–86, 112
Trader Josh Trading Room,
189–194, 196
daily chart room, 190, 191, 192
fusion trading, 192
swing-trading room, 190,
192–194
Trader Josh Training Program,
195–199
FASTKEY order execution, 199
inclusions in program, 199
learning objectives, 197–198
program details, 196–197
reasons for developing, 195
screen hardware
recommendation, 54,
104–105
time required, 196
Trading hours, 19, 77, 169
Training/coaching, 187–199. *See
also* Demo (paper) trading
in controlling impatience, 9
for earnings release trading, 186
for fusion trading, 196–197,
201–205
importance of, 32, 173–175,
201–205
for intra-day trading, 107,
140–142

net profit as goal, 174–175
100-share-block trades in, 3–4,
13–14, 16
for pivot trading, 178, 186
potential scams, 38–39, 189,
196
practicing with intra-day setups,
85–86
screen hardware
recommendation, 54,
104–105
for sideline trading, 186
Trader Josh Trading Room,
189–194, 196
Trader Josh Training Program,
195–199
Transparency, 24, 190

Volatility:
from government regulation,
36–37
from news and economic
reports, 5, 21, 37
stock price and, 35

Whiteboard logs:
contents, 68–70
fusion trading, 150, 151, 153,
157–158, 167
intra-day trading, 68–74
swing trading, 144, 154,
161–163
Wick, of candlestick charts,
55, 56

Yahoo Finance, 29

INDEX